Oracle Wait Event Tuning

High Performance with Wait Event Interface Analysis

Stephen Andert

This book is dedicated to my wife, Deanna whose love and support made this book possible.

-Stephen Andert

Oracle Wait Event Tuning
High Performance with Wait Event Interface Analysis

By Stephen Andert

Copyright © 2004 by Rampant TechPress. All rights reserved.

Printed in the United States of America.

Published in Kittrell, North Carolina, USA.

Oracle In-focus Series: Book 22

Series Editor: Don Burleson

Editors: Kelly Gay, Janet Burleson, John Lavender, Robin Haden, Teri Wade

Production Editor: Teri Wade

Cover Design: Bryan Hoff

Illustrations: Mike Reed

Printing History: October 2004 for First Edition

ISBN: 0-9745993-7-9

Library of Congress Control Number: 2004096474

Table of Contents

Table of Contents

Using the Online Code Depot

Purchase of this book provides complete access to the online code depot that contains the sample code scripts.

All of the code depot scripts in this book are located at the following URL:

rampant.cc/wait.htm

All of the code scripts in this book are available for download in zip format, ready to load and use.

If technical assistance is needed in downloading or accessing the scripts, please contact Rampant TechPress at info@rampant.cc.

Advanced Oracle Monitoring and Tuning Script Collection

The complete collection from Mike Ault, the world's best DBA.

Packed with 590 ready-to-use Oracle scripts, this is the definitive collection for every Oracle professional DBA.

It would take many years to develop these scripts from scratch, making this download the best value in the Oracle industry.

It's only $39.95 (less than 7 cents per script!)

To buy for immediate download, go to

http://www.oracle-script.com

Conventions Used in this Book

It is critical for any technical publication to follow rigorous standards and employ consistent punctuation conventions to make the text easy to read.

However, this is not an easy task. Within Oracle there are many types of notation that can confuse a reader. Some Oracle utilities such as STATSPACK and TKPROF are always spelled in CAPITAL letters, while Oracle parameters and procedures have varying naming conventions in the Oracle documentation. It is also important to remember that many Oracle commands are case sensitive, and are always left in their original executable form, and never altered with italics or capitalization.

Hence, all Rampant TechPress books follow these conventions:

Parameters - All Oracle parameters will be lowercase italics. Exceptions to this rule are parameter arguments that are commonly capitalized (KEEP pool, TKPROF), these will be left in ALL CAPS.

Variables – All PL/SQL program variables and arguments will also remain in lowercase italics (*dbms_job*, *dbms_utility*).

Tables & dictionary objects – All data dictionary objects are referenced in lowercase italics (*dba_indexes*, *v$sql*). This includes all *v$* and *x$* views (*x$kcbcbh*, *v$parameter*) and dictionary views (*dba_tables*, *user_indexes*).

SQL – All SQL is formatted for easy use in the code depot, and all SQL is displayed in lowercase. The main SQL terms (select, from, where, group by, order by, having) will always appear on a separate line.

Programs & Products – All products and programs that are known to the author are capitalized according to the vendor specifications (IBM, DBXray, etc). All names known by Rampant TechPress to be trademark names appear in this text as initial caps. References to UNIX are always made in uppercase.

Acknowledgements

It is incredibly rewarding to see a project like this progress from a vision that can fit on a 3 by 5 card to a bound and printed book. Any writing endeavor of this size cannot be accomplished without many people putting in a lot of hard work. A word of thanks seems to be small reward indeed, but my gratitude needs to be expressed to all the people that have played a role in this project.

Technical reviewers and copy editors helped polish my rough drafts, verify technical and grammatical accuracy and added insight to many areas. In particular, Jeff Markham provided timely feedback and suggestions that helped me keep things on the right track and on topic; Kevin Hedger provided another perspective and added some of the material found in the Code Depot to help analyze data; Tom Parkinson and Mladen Googla also made valuable contributions to make this a better book. Finally, Cindy Cairns worked copy-editing magic that made this a much better book than it was before her input. They all found things that helped make this a better book, but remember any errors that may linger are not their fault, but mine.

It was good to work with Rampant staff like Linda, John, Don and Janet who believed in me and this project and were there every step of the way to help and encourage me and even to nudge me along when schedules started to get tight.

Throughout this process, colleagues at work and friends from church have been very supportive. Even when the mere mention of Oracle makes their eyes glaze over, they have been encouraging and supportive.

Finally, my family has been extremely supportive and I have to thank my wonderful wife Deanna for all the extra tasks she has taken on during this project that allowed me the necessary time to make this book happen. My boys, Kevin and Timothy, have been more understanding that I deserve and have put up with my frequent "quiet times" when meeting deadlines. Thank you all.

Stephen Andert

Preface

There are many books about Oracle available today, so what is different about this one? Several things make this book deserve a spot on the Oracle professional's bookshelf. Not the least of which is that this book is not trying to cover every aspect and nuance of the Oracle RDBMS; it is focused on tuning. Within the Oracle database tuning arena, the traditional approach has been to use various hit ratios and a checklist. This approach led to a typical tuning process going something like this: First, check ratio X. If too low/high, modify setting Y until the ratio is good. If users are still reporting problems with performance, check something else and tune the appropriate parameters or settings until the statistic looked good. This process would continue until the users were happy with performance or the DBA ran out of items on their checklist and declared the problem solved by virtue of the database being tuned as much as possible.

This process worked often enough that it gained widespread acceptance. However, there is a better way. The Wait Interface allows a DBA to look at exactly what resource is hindering performance. Instead of a checklist, this approach is a laser beam pointer to quickly identify the solution.

This book is designed for everyone ranging from the new DBA who is facing their first performance-tuning problem to the experienced DBA who gained their experience with solving tuning problems with the checklist approach or by using ratios. There are merits to some ratio tuning approaches; this book will show you *when* to use them instead of just presenting a checklist in a new order with a few new twists.

Stephen Andert

Database Tuning Approaches

What Is Tuning?

Tuning a database is an activity with the goal of making the database run better than it did before. This is like tuning an automobile to make it run smoother, get better gas mileage or make it go faster. There are established guidelines that are used for tuning a car or truck. For every few thousand miles, it is recommended that the oil, air filter, transmission fluid, spark plugs, belts and hoses be inspected or changed. These tune-ups are in the category of routine maintenance. In a database, routine maintenance covers things like analyzing statistics and rebuilding indexes if certain conditions are met. With a car, it is generally recommended that the oil be changed every 3000 miles. With a database, indexes with a blevel that is greater than 4 require rebuilding. These types of "rules of thumb" are what most DBAs use for tuning.

Some database tuning rules have been developed through testing and analysis of results. Others are "guesstimates" with no foundation in fact. Some of these rules work consistently while others work under certain conditions. However, as Oracle evolved over time, guesstimates became less effective and less meaningful.

This book will introduce options which allow more success in maintaining database performance without embarking on a wild goose chase. Many of today's leading technologists have researched performance and made insightful discoveries. The presentations, articles and white papers that they have produced reveal straightforward ways to tune today's complex Oracle databases. This book will put these fundamental lessons together in a practical way. In the appendix, a list of resources for the research that has been conducted contributing to the information contained in this book will be provided.

Why Tuning Is Needed

Oracle databases are complicated creatures requiring much care and maintenance. Even a small database will, with time and use, grow in size and complexity. A process or report that once performed with an adequate run-time will run more slowly the longer the system is in use. This is due to more demands being made on the system as well as the increasing amount of data through which the systems needs to search to perform operations. All too often, this happens gradually until the users have a critical deadline that will be missed because the payroll report that used to run in 45 minutes is now taking 2 hours. This realization triggers a reactive tuning session as the DBA attempts to respond to the sudden demand to increase database performance.

"I believe I may have a crisis here"

It is the DBA's job to maintain and improve database performance, even before a crisis. This is accomplished through proactive tuning. This book addresses new ways for the DBA to identify the causes of database application performance problems. Methodologies will be presented for finding solutions to poor performance problems. In addition, proactive tuning can help keep performance in line with forecast increases in usage.

How to Tune?

There are many ways to tune a database. Some of them are good ways to improve the performance of the database. Other ways may be less successful, and may only help to line the pockets of hardware vendors.

One of the ways to tune a database is using ratios. With database tuning, ratios come into play with the difference between finding something typically in memory and not finding it, which requires an I/O from disk. For example, an SQL query might look for 10,000 data blocks. If 9,000 of these blocks can be found in the buffer cache, then the other 1,000 blocks must be read from disk. In this example, the query has a 90% buffer cache hit ratio.

Another way to tune a database is using the wait interface. The fundamental guideline that drives this methodology is that whatever the database is spending the most time waiting on is the bottleneck. By fixing the bottleneck, performance can increase to the level of the next bottleneck; which by definition is now larger than the current one, so performance must get better.

The difference between these two approaches is analogous to treating the symptoms of the problem rather than treating the underlying cause of the problem.

Ratios – Historical Introduction

Tuning has always been an important part of a DBA's job, ranking right next to backup and recovery. It has often been viewed as "black magic." That perception originated from the tuning process that was taught by many experts and touted in the many books on tuning. That process centered on using ratios to determine the health of a database or component of the database.

According to the ratio school of thought, if the Buffer Cache Hit Ratio (BCHR) is too low, then the size of the buffer cache should be increased to improve performance. If this fixed the problem and the database ran better, then the DBA was awarded guru status and managers would likely follow almost any recommendations made. If these changes showed no improvement or made things worse, another DBA would be brought in. The new DBA might determine that another ratio was out of line and make a different change, or simply increase the magnitude of the initial changes. If this change made performance better, then the new DBA became the guru.

This school of thought is based, at least in part, on the rationale that it is faster to access data blocks from memory (RAM) than from disk. Therefore, if too many data blocks were being read from disk, then a possible cause of performance degradation is the buffer cache being too small to keep enough data blocks available for the users. Usually, the solution to that problem was to increase the buffer cache.

To better understand ratios, it may help to illustrate using a non-database example. Theoretically it is faster to get to work if there are no stoplights to wait for. So to reduce commute time, try and reduce the time spent at stoplights. One way would be to simply keep going even when the lights are red, but that could get dangerous and cause increased insurance premiums, so another way would be to tune or change the commute. See Figure 1.1 for the initial commute.

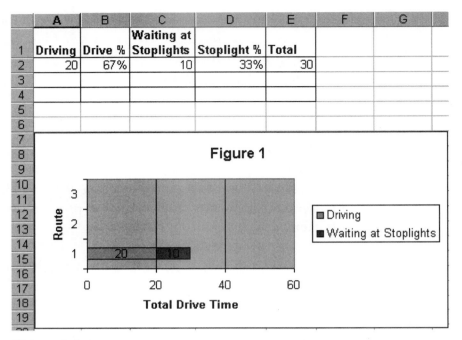

Figure 1.1 – *Breakdown of Tome for Initial Commute*

30 minutes to get to work =
20 minutes driving +
10 minutes waiting for stoplights

About 67% of the time is spent driving and 33% is spent waiting for stoplights. Assuming that waiting for lights is the stoplight miss ratio (SLMR), then striving for a lower percentage of time waiting for lights would seem logical. The rationale for using this ratio as a measurement is the assumption that missing a green light makes the commute longer, so a lower SLMR theoretically means getting to or from work faster. This would mean less time to get to work, but the ratio tuning methodology does not specify or measure that metric. Figure 1.2 depicts the commute with a newly devised route to work that is longer but with less stop lights.

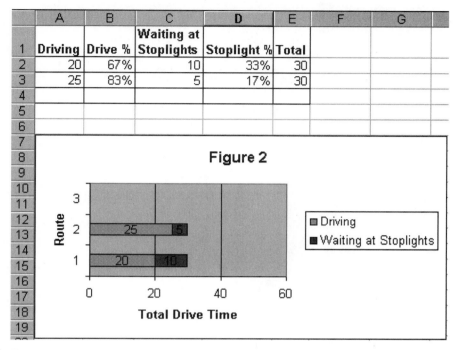

	A	B	C	D	E	F	G
1	Driving	Drive %	Waiting at Stoplights	Stoplight %	Total		
2	20	67%	10	33%	30		
3	25	83%	5	17%	30		
4							
5							
6							

Figure 1.2 – *Comparison of Initial Commute and First "Tuned" Commute*

30 minutes to get to work =
25 minutes driving +
5 minutes waiting for traffic lights

In this case, about 83% of the time is spent driving and 17% waiting for traffic lights. The traffic light miss ratio has improved, however the total commute took the same amount of time as before, but now requires more distance resulting is more miles and greater gas consumption each day.

Since this still does not accomplish the objective of getting home or to work quicker, trying to find another way might be in order. Figure 1.3 shows another way with less stop lights.

	A	B	C	D	E	F	G
1	Driving	Drive %	Waiting at Stoplights	Stoplight %	Total		
2	20	67%	10	33%	30		
3	25	83%	5	17%	30		
4	40	89%	5	11%	45		
5							
6							
7							
8							
9							
10							
11							
12							
13							
14							
15							
16							
17							
18							
19							

Figure 3

Route

Driving
Waiting at Stoplights

Total Drive Time

Figure 1.3 – *Breakdown of Third Commute*

45 minutes to get to work =
40 minutes driving +
5 minutes waiting for traffic lights

This time, about 89% of the time is spent driving and 11% waiting for traffic lights. The traffic light miss ratio has now dropped to 11%, which is much better than the original 33%. Unfortunately, the commute now takes 50% longer and is a lot longer in distance. The SLMR metric is improving, but not quite hitting the mark of getting home or to work sooner.

This illustration helps to show one of the flaws in tuning by ratios. Improving these metrics may not always resolve the poor performance the user sees. Unfortunately, for quite some time, that was the common knowledge and what any DBA that went to training, seminars or sat at the feet of the guru's learned. The hit-or-miss results obtained by following the ratio philosophy have muddied the waters. Some people claimed success by doing this hit-and-miss ratio philosophy, and then wrote books and gave seminars on the practice, when others followed the same steps and saw no positive change. Sometimes the problem was a buffer cache that was undersized, and the low Buffer Cache Hit Ratio (BCHR) really *was* accurately measuring the problem. By increasing the buffer cache, there would be less data blocks that needed to be read from disk, which would result in better performance. Other times, the problem was that the network was too slow and the delays the users were complaining about were not a database problem. Moreover, maybe a user had started running a query that was performing multiple full table-scans on the largest table. The possible causes of a slow database are many and unfortunately, the ratio methodology cannot identify a lot of them.

Another problem with the ratio method is mathematical. The following three ratios are all the same, but they have different values for the components of the formula.

10/100=0.1
100/1000=0.1
1000/10000=0.1

All three of these ratios are 10%. If a job offer came with a tax-to-salary rate of 10%, which monthly paycheck would be preferred? $10,000 per month sounds much better than $1,000 per month. In database terms, in the case of the BCHR, a high value ratio could mean that the database is very efficient and is almost never reading from disk. Or it could mean that the database is reading some things from the buffer cache far more often than it needs to. A small code adjustment could bring the hit ratio down but increase the performance due to the reduction in data that needs to be read.

Examining trends can be insightful in database administration. For example, observing that database space usage is growing at a rate of 4 GB each month, to say that 20 GB of free space will only last 5 months is a simple exercise. In tuning, trend analysis can help identify the existence of a problem. For example, a BCHR that suddenly drops from an average of 90% to 60% indicates there could potentially be a problem. While there is some discussion about the validity of certain ratios for trending database performance and identifying deviations from normal to help identify problems, this book will not be discussing ratios in any great detail.

Another issue with ratios is that these values take a while after startup to be reliable. This is due to the fact that when the database is first started, none of the data blocks are in the buffer cache until they are first accessed. This means that until a normal load has been placed on the database for a period of time, these ratios are not reliable.

The problem with ratios is that bad ratios are not the problem. Bad ratios are an incomplete and sometimes misleading measure of an underlying issue. This is the basic flaw of the ratio tuning methodology.

Wait Interface – A New Approach

For the past couple of years, this was the state of affairs for database administrators. Simply tune by ratios and hope for the best. In the past several years, however, a new methodology has started picking up steam. It is frequently called the Wait Interface movement and loyal adherents to this system appear to be afraid to even use the word ratio. Wait Interface simply refers to the mechanism by which the DBA can interface with the database to see where it is spending its time, whether that time is waiting or working. If a large amount of time is spent waiting for a resource, this might be an indicator of why the users are calling complaining about performance.

Skepticism reigned as the topic of Wait Interface surfaced at a user conference. After all, Oracle wasn't making the presentations and it just seemed too good to be true. Gaja Vadyanatha's presentation, *Myths and Folklore IOUG Live! 2001*, changed all that. Understanding the practical application of the Wait Interface was the key to understanding this new approach. This new approach was different from the holy grail of ratio tuning and frequently seemed a mirage. For example, why would increase the buffer cache if the slow response time is being caused by an overloaded disk controller or inefficient SQL statements?

The Wait Interface was introduced to the Oracle code several versions ago in Oracle 7 and has become more reliable and robust with each version and release. Over time, it has gained more attention and with that, better understanding of how to use it to tune performance. It consists of dynamic performance views which are primarily *v$system_event,* *v$session_event,* *v$session_wait* and *v$event_name*.

Since the arrival of Windows in the computer world, interface is usually associated with graphical, as in Graphical User Interface (GUI). Therefore, the name *wait interface* implies a method of access to look at the waits in the database. However, there is nothing graphical about this interface. In fact, the dynamic performance views that are used are simply views into the system statistics. SQL queries are used to examine these views to see where the database is spending its time. There are some vendors and others in the open source world that have created GUI tools to access the wait interface and others have enhanced their products to include screens to look at the wait events. These are handy resources, but it is important to understand the foundational concepts. Knowing what the wait events are available and how to fix them is more important than whether to use a set of scripts from the Internet or a licensed tool with lots of flashing colors.

To better understand the wait interface the commuting example from earlier will be used in the hopes that it may illustrate the concepts using a real-world scenario:

30 minutes to get to work =
20 minutes driving +
10 minutes waiting for traffic lights

In this case, since the drive time is the biggest component of the commute, start looking there for ways to shorten drive time. If drive time is increased because of the use of side streets, maybe adding a few miles to the trip in order to use a freeway might reduce the drive time since the speed limit is higher. Perhaps the freeway is more like a parking lot since everyone else uses the same route at the same time. Going into work 45 minutes earlier could cut drive time by 25%. Maybe a new engine will enhance performance since the current one has trouble keeping up with the speed limit. The moral of that story is that there is no standard answer using ratio methodology so it is necessary to look at the big picture. Notice that unlike the earlier stoplight ratio-tuning example, the first component under investigation is drive time, not time at stoplights.

When using the wait interface and after identifying the largest chunk of time, that becomes the first target for enhancement. If most of the time is spent in file I/O operations, it probably does not make any sense to try and tune the library cache. This approach is one of the 2 main approaches that will be discussed in this book. This concept was not mentioned in a Performance Tuning class from Oracle Education a few years ago. Rumor has it that the class is being retooled to address wait-based tuning. The wait-interface approach is valuable because it unambiguously tells where the database is hurting which allows changes to be made to have the biggest positive impact on performance.

10046 Tracing

10046 tracing refers to setting event 10046 to a specific non-zero value in order to obtain information about a session. Oracle Note 218105.1 states that events are primarily used to produce additional diagnostic information when insufficient information is available to resolve a given problem. In this case, event 10046 will help identify what a session is doing and provide insight as to why it is taking longer than the user would like. That same note also warns, "Do not use an Oracle Diagnostic Event unless directed to do so by Oracle Support Services or via a Support related article on Metalink." In general, it is true that experimenting with different values for some events could cause headaches of massive proportions. In this case, enough other experts have determined how this event works and how to use it safely in performance tuning activities that the directions in this book or other articles from reputable sources, such as Steve Adams www.ixora.com.au, and Cary Millsap www.hotsos.com, should be good resources. Part of the warning is due to the verbosity of the files produced by enabling this event. The files that are generated can easily fill a mount point if care is not taken. Setting this event to level 8 or 12 as directed in this book will provide wait information that will help identify the bottleneck for a process.

"I wonder if 10046 tracing could help sort this out."

The wait interface provides the ability to look at the whole database and see who and what are the largest time-consumers. By the way, 10046 tracing is sometimes pronounced, "one-hundred-forty-six tracing" instead of saying "ten-thousand-forty-six tracing," which would be correct. However said, it addresses the question of troubleshooting one specific session to see why it is taking so long to run. When it seems like everyone in the company is calling to ask why the database is so slow, don't expect to respond that, based on 10046 the database is slow because of X. 10046 allows the review of one user session to determine what is making that particular session slow. After identifying a key user whose process must be made faster first, tackle that process with a 10046 trace. This trace can be set at various levels that start from a level 1 SQL Trace as shown in Figure 1.4.

```
SQL> alter session set events '10046 trace name context forever
level 1';

Session altered.

SQL> select * from customer
  2  where name like '%Ellis%';

NAME
-------------------------------
Larry Ellison

SQL> alter session set events '10046 trace name context off';

Session altered.
```

Figure 1.4 – *Example of Starting and Stopping a 10046 Trace*

This basic level trace produces information like what is shown below in Figure 1.5.

```
PARSING IN CURSOR #1 len=48 dep=0 uid=25 oct=3 lid=25 tim=1036141712032927 hv=2681671403
select * from customer
where name like '%Ellis%'
END OF STMT
PARSE #1:c=10000,e=51777,p=0,cr=0,cu=0,mis=1,r=0,dep=0,og=4,tim=1036141712032860
EXEC #1:c=0,e=285,p=0,cr=0,cu=0,mis=0,r=0,dep=0,og=4,tim=1036141712034381
FETCH #1:c=0,e=979,p=0,cr=16,cu=0,mis=0,r=1,dep=0,og=4,tim=1036141712035791
FETCH #1:c=10000,e=269,p=0,cr=2,cu=0,mis=0,r=0,dep=0,og=4,tim=1036141712038210
*** 2003-08-15 21:45:26.644
```

Figure 1.5 – *Sample Trace File*

This example is using the lowest level of detail, and would really be primarily useful when tracing another user's session wanting to see what SQL they were running. The example demonstrates that the trace file identifies the SQL that the session was running. Greater levels of detail exist and will be discussed in future chapters.

Most of the information contained in Figure 1.5 probably looks like gibberish right now. That is OK, since Chapter 3 covers generating trace files in detail and then Chapter 6 covers how to use and interpret them. For now, suffice it to say that using

10046 trace is like going to the doctor and providing the doctor with a list of the pain levels, temperatures and blood flow rates. The doctor will not need to ask as he will have the data necessary to identify the ailment. He will diagnose the problem quickly, prescribe the appropriate treatment and, hopefully, cure the problem soon.

Gathering Real-Time System Waits Events

The wait-based analysis method discussed so far is the 10046 trace events. Another way of using waits to tune database performance is to use real-time system wait events. Wait Events are the events that are causing the database system to wait or not complete work as quickly as otherwise possible. These events are recorded by the system as they happen, or in real time. There are plenty of *v$* views that contain information about waits. For example, a simple query on an OLTP database with several hundred concurrent sessions would look like this:

```
select
   event ,
   count(*)
from
   v$session_wait
group by
   event
order by
   2;
```

EVENT	COUNT(*)
SQL*Net more data from client	1
db file scattered read	1
null event	1
pmon timer	1
smon timer	1
rdbms ipc message	7
SQL*Net message from client	159

Figure 1.6 – *Sample v$session_wait data*

This gives a count of how many occurrences of each type of wait have occurred recently. There are 2 problems with this query. The first is that knowing how many times a given wait has happened provides nothing useful about how long the session has waited. Knowing that there were 7 waits for "rdbms ipc message" does not mean that is what is making the system slow. Going back to the commuting example, it would be like saying "there were 10 red lights." The wait for each light could vary in length.

The second problem is that this data is of very short duration. Constant monitoring would be necessary to capture the waits that are causing the users to complain. These problems highlight the importance of understanding the methodology behind the tools. Someone with a basic understanding of the wait interface could start making tuning decisions using the value returned by the above query.

One way to overcome this problem is to capture this information and save it periodically to a table that can be referenced to see what was going on at an earlier time. There are various ways to accomplish this. Each way has its own advantages and drawbacks.

STATSPACK

Another way to capture useful information on waits is using STATSPACK. STATSPACK is a set of scripts, which allow the collection, automation, storage, review and clean up of performance data. This is the replacement of the *utlbstat.sql* and *utlestat.sql* scripts from earlier releases of Oracle. These scripts produced a report that has been used for tuning activities for several major releases of Oracle. These scripts are still there, but the benefits of STATSPACK are so numerous, that it is much more commonly used. STATSPACK can be used on any database 8.0.5 and later, although 8.0 users do not have the script with the database and will need to obtain it separately.

One of the issues that made utlbstat/utlestat challenging was that it was required to run one script to start a measurement period and another to end. This activity produced a file that could then be analyzed to identify potential performance issues. This was a problem since the snapshot was for a given time period, and all analysis had to be done based on that period. Obtaining a larger or smaller time frame including that period was not an option. STATSPACK allows a "snapshot" of statistics to be obtained at 15-minute intervals for 4 hours, for example. This allows review of any period from 15 minutes through 4 hours in 15-minute increments. This is helpful if after looking at a 4-hour window, more detail is desired. It allows the review of appropriate reporting windows in smaller sizes until the 15-minute interval that has the most-preferred information is reached.

Another benefit of STATSPACK that is significant for many organizations is that it comes free with Oracle. With the proper knowledge, this tool can provide information that is vital to any DBA attempting to resolve any performance problem.

Conclusion

This chapter has introduced database-tuning concepts and discussed the two main approaches to tuning, ratios and waits. It has also provided a brief overview of several of the tools available in the wait events analysis camp:

- 10046 trace
- real-time wait analysis
- STATSPACK.

By now it is clear that using ratios to tune a database is not always productive and it is necessary to start digging into other options. The next chapters will cover more ground on the topic of wait events and analysis, and will start showing some useful methodologies that will help the DBA remain the tuning guru in the office instead of the goat.

Wait Interface – An elapsed-time measurement system

Introduction

When the users start calling in death threats because "the database is slow," it pays to have something that can be used to find out why so the problem can be fixed quickly. This is more challenging than it may seem at first since there are many components in today's complex systems. Is the problem with the user's pc, their local area network, the application server, the link between the application server and the database server or the database itself? If the application is Web-based, then add to that list of possible suspects the wide-area network, the internet and the web server. If the problem is in the database itself, is it the buffer cache not containing enough information for quick retrieval, execution plans being aged out of the shared pool, locking or latching issues, excessive parsing or any of the myriad of other components in today's Oracle RDMS.

"The database is too slow!"

The Wait Interface is one way to identify from the database where the problem that is affecting the users is located. For example, if the Wait Interface indicates a problem with I/O operations (db file sequential read), then there is probably a storage problem. It would make sense to work with the system administration group to see what can be done to alleviate the I/O bottleneck. Other causes, such as bad SQL or bad statistics, could be causing unnecessary full table scans. Consequently, it is important to understand the Wait Interface and what it is revealing about the entire system, both inside and outside of the database.

Background

The Wait Interface started to appear in the Oracle RDBMS in version 7. However, the Wait Interface first started to become more widely known with Anjo Kolk's YAPP (*Yet Another Performance Profiling*) Method paper published in 1999. Since that time, many more people have written about it in technical white papers and articles and spoken about it at user groups and conferences.

So, What is the Wait Interface?

Wait Interface is the name that has been given to the mechanism in an Oracle database that allows the DBA to look into the internal workings. This allows the DBA to see what various components are doing by looking at where they are spending their time waiting. While some wait-related information can be gathered by other views, the three main views that examine the Wait Interface are:

- *v$system_event*

- *v$session_event*

- *v$session_wait*

Why are these three views the key? A review of what information they each contain and a sample of their output may help illustrate their importance. Remember to enable timed statistics in the database by using the *timed_statistics*=TRUE parameter in the *init.ora* file or *spfile* or by altering the system using:

```
ALTER SYSTEM SET TIMED_STATISTICS = TRUE;
```

Otherwise, there will be no timing information. Oracle says there is a small impact on the system when this is turned on, but most agree that anyone on any recent Oracle version should generally leave this on all the time. In theory, there may be a performance penalty for a mechanical speedometer in a car, but that doesn't mean people looking for optimum performance remove their speedometer. The information provided by the speedometer more than offsets its small performance impact. Likewise, the performance impact of enabling *timed_statistics* compared to the availability of better information on how the database is performing.

Before Oracle 9i, the default setting for this was FALSE, but by 8i, the majority of DBA's agreed that the cost was negligible and set this value to TRUE everywhere, including in their production environments. As of Oracle 9i, it seems that Oracle Corporation agrees since the default is now TRUE.

v$system_event

The highest-level view is *v$system_event*. Its structure is shown in Figure 2.1 below:

```
SQL > desc v$system_event

Name                    Null?    Type
--------------------    --------  ---------------
EVENT                            VARCHAR2(64)
TOTAL_WAITS                      NUMBER
TOTAL_TIMEOUTS                   NUMBER
TIME_WAITED                      NUMBER
AVERAGE_WAIT                     NUMBER
TIME_WAITED_MICRO                NUMBER
```

Figure 2.1 – *Describe v$system_event*

Here are explanations of some of the more important fields:

- EVENT is the name of the event that is taking time.

- TOTAL_WAITS represents the total number of times this event has caused a process to wait.

- TIME_WAITED is the total number of *centiseconds* that processes have waited for this event.

- AVERAGE_WAIT is effectively the result of TIME_WAITED divided by TOTAL_WAITS.

In addition, there are a few pieces of information to be aware.

First of all, not all events are worthy of attention in this view. Some of the wait events that occur in a database can be ignored when looking at the whole system. These are usually referred to as *idle events* since they usually do not occur unless the database is idle or waiting for work. Theoretically, these events are not preventing any work from getting done and therefore could not possibly be performance bottlenecks. An important thing to remember about idle events is that although sometimes they are treated as idle or not important, it is possible to increase the accuracy of measurement of these events so that it is possible to determine if they are truly idle or if they might be contributing or pointing out a performance problem.

For example, SQL*Net message from client is an event that can occur when the client session is idle or waiting for commands from the application or user. This is sometimes called user think time and would be considered idle time. This event can also be seen when a session is running a batch job and has no user prompts or interaction, which would possibly make this an important wait event that could be indicative of a network related bottleneck. In this case, it would not be an idle event and overlooking it could mean focusing attention elsewhere instead of working on the problem at hand.

Secondly, keep in mind that *v$system_event* is *cumulative*. That is to say that it simply keeps adding counts or time to the events as they have occurred since the instance was started. This means that if the database has been up for 100 days, when looking at data from this view, be aware that it lumps data from today in with data from 100 days ago and every day in between. This will decrease the chances that any bottlenecks will stand out consequently averages over long periods of time lose their meaning. For example, the database may have had an absolutely horrid problem with "db file sequential read" waits on a particular day, but not on others. In this case, the waits for "db

Oracle Wait Event Tuning

file sequential read" would be smoothed out so that the problem really doesn't stand out.

To provide an idea what the data in this view looks like, here is a sample of some data that was generated using the script *show_system_events.sql*.

🖫 show_system_events.sql

```
-- ****************************************************
-- Copyright © 2003 by Rampant TechPress
-- This script is free for non-commercial purposes
-- with no warranties.  Use at your own risk.
--
-- To license this script for a commercial purpose,
-- contact info@rampant.cc
-- ****************************************************

/* show_system_events.sql */
select
   EVENT,
   TOTAL_WAITS "TOT WAITS",
   TIME_WAITED "TIME WAITED",
   AVERAGE_WAIT "AVG"
from
   V$SYSTEM_EVENT
where
   EVENT not in (
      select EVENT from STATS$IDLE_EVENT
      )
order by
   TIME_WAITED desc;
```

EVENT	TOT WAITS	TIME WAITED	AVG
control file parallel write	89888	73256	1
free buffer waits	9152	66127	7
enqueue	3306	48480	15
log buffer space	7889	41294	5
db file sequential read	80446	40005	0
log file sync	5934	29038	5
write complete waits	604	22173	37
buffer busy waits	4029	19930	5
db file scattered read	16072	8670	1
rdbms ipc reply	291	7564	26
log file switch completion	541	5706	11
log file parallel write	28672	5593	0
latch free	1488	3109	2
control file sequential read	38644	2548	0
undo segment extension	308003	743	0
LGWR wait for redo copy	3116	482	0
control file heartbeat	1	399	399
library cache pin	2	393	196
log file single write	320	306	1
db file parallel read	9	112	12
log file switch (checkpoint incomplete) 3		106	35

Figure 2.2 – *v$system_event by TIME_WAITED*

Figure 2.2 is the output of the *show_system_events.sql* script. It illustrates that the database spent the most time waiting for the control file parallel write. If instead of total time waited, average amount of time waited is viewed by changing the order by clause in the previous query to AVERAGE_WAIT desc, the wait for control file parallel write is several orders of magnitude smaller than the other average waits. Refer to the report in Figure 2.3.

Oracle Wait Event Tuning

EVENT	TOT WAITS	TIME WAITED	AVG
control file heartbeat	1	399	399
library cache pin	2	393	196
write complete waits	604	22173	37
log file switch (checkpoint incomplete)	3	106	35
rdbms ipc reply	291	7564	26
process startup	6	90	15
enqueue	3306	48480	15
db file parallel read	9	112	12
log file switch completion	541	5706	11
reliable message	1	7	7
refresh controlfile command	1	7	7
free buffer waits	9152	66127	7
buffer busy waits	4029	19930	5
log file sync	5934	29038	5
log buffer space	7889	41294	5
latch free	1488	3109	2
checkpoint completed	1	2	2
control file parallel write	90000	73329	1
db file scattered read	16072	8670	1
db file single write	12	8	1
index block split	19	22	1
log file single write	320	306	1

Figure 2.3 – *v$system_event by AVERAGE_WAIT*

Tuning, even up the point of eliminating, control file parallel write waits would not have made a noticeable difference to the users. The biggest target when looking at the AVERAGE_WAIT column becomes the control file heartbeat. Since this event only happened one time, unless this wait was a contributing factor in a performance complaint, it is probably safe to ignore this since it could have taken place at any time since this database instance was started. The problem with the *v$system_event* is evidenced by the fact that an event could have only happened at one point in time and stopped causing a problem. *v$system_event* should be used by looking at the deltas, or differences in values between two fairly short snapshots. This means that the query sample will need to be a bit more complex.

The first script in this series is designed to take a picture of the data contained in *v$system_event*. This will help determine which events are currently creating the performance issues. It is called *start_system_events.sql*.

🖫 start_system_events.sql

```
--  ************************************************
-- Copyright © 2003 by Rampant TechPress
-- This script is free for non-commercial purposes
-- with no warranties.  Use at your own risk.
--
-- To license this script for a commercial purpose,
-- contact info@rampant.cc
--  ************************************************

/* start_system_events.sql    */
/* Clean-up from any prior runs */
drop table start_system;

/* create working table */
create
   table start_system
   as select
      *
   from
      v$system_event
   where
      1=2;

/* Populate the start table */
insert into START_SYSTEM
select
   *
from
   v$system_event;
```

After running this script, wait for a period of time to let the database track some work. Try and time the running of these scripts at a time when the database is active. After an appropriate amount of time, run the script, *finish_system_events.sql* to capture the end status of the *v$system_event* data.

💾 finish_system_events.sql

```
-- ****************************************************
-- Copyright © 2003 by Rampant TechPress
-- This script is free for non-commercial purposes
-- with no warranties.  Use at your own risk.
--
-- To license this script for a commercial purpose,
-- contact info@rampant.cc
-- ****************************************************

/* finish_system_events.sql    */
/* Clean-up from any prior runs */
drop table FINISH_SYSTEM;

/* create working table */
create
   table FINISH_SYSTEM
   as select
      *
   from
     V$SYSTEM_EVENT
   where
     1=2;

/* Populate the finish table */
insert
   into FINISH_SYSTEM
   select
      *
   from
     V$SYSTEM_EVENT;
```

As soon as this script finishes, run *difference_system_events.sql* to obtain the difference in the event values between the start and finish scripts.

💾 difference_system_events.sql

```
-- ****************************************************
-- Copyright © 2003 by Rampant TechPress
-- This script is free for non-commercial purposes
-- with no warranties.  Use at your own risk.
--
-- To license this script for a commercial purpose,
-- contact info@rampant.cc
-- ****************************************************

/* difference_system_events.sql  */
```

```
/* With a little subtraction (finish minus start) we can see what
was going on in the database for the time we measured. */
col event form a35
select
   a.EVENT,
   b.TOTAL_WAITS    - a.TOTAL_WAITS "WAITS",
   b.TOTAL_TIMEOUTS - a.TOTAL_TIMEOUTS "TIMEOUTS",
   b.TIME_WAITED    - a.TIME_WAITED "TIME WAITED",
   b.AVERAGE_WAIT   - a.AVERAGE_WAIT "AVG WAIT"
from
   START_SYSTEM a,
   FINISH_SYSTEM b
where
   a.EVENT = b.EVENT
order by
   "AVG WAIT",
   "TIME WAITED";
```

EVENT	WAITS	TIMEOUTS	TIME WAITED	AVG WAIT
buffer busy waits	317	0	1232	0
write complete waits	72	7	2563	0
log file sync	571	1	3192	0
log buffer space	900	0	4219	0
pmon timer	72	72	20867	0
enqueue	360	11	6982	1
SQL*Net message from client	5	0	20868	2
rdbms ipc reply	63	9	2011	10
library cache pin	1	1	299	102

Figure 2.4 – *v$system_event for a time period*

Figure 2.4 shows the output from running this query for a several minute interval. There were 2 active sessions as well as other idle sessions. If the results indicate that several of the top events are related to I/O, then there is probably an I/O bottleneck. If the results indicate buffer busy waits, then a bigger buffer cache or more efficient SQL may be in order. Chapters 5 through 7 cover how to deal with the specific bottlenecks.

Also, note that this view is different depending on the version of Oracle. There is one difference in this table in version 8i as compared to version 9i. The TIME_WAITED_MICRO field is a new field in version 9i added to allow measurements as a more granular level. It measures the amount of time that processes have waited, just like the TIME_WAITED field. The difference is that this new field measures time in microseconds.

v$system_event contains valuable information on what the whole database is doing. But that is only a starting place. It is necessary to dig down deeper and examine the specific causes of the bottlenecks. *v$session_event* provides that information.

v$session_event

```
SQL> desc v$session_event
 Name                    Null? Type
 ----------------------- ----- ----------------
 SID                           NUMBER
 EVENT                         VARCHAR2(64)
 TOTAL_WAITS                   NUMBER
 TOTAL_TIMEOUTS                NUMBER
 TIME_WAITED                   NUMBER
 AVERAGE_WAIT                  NUMBER
 MAX_WAIT                      NUMBER
 TIME_WAITED_MICRO             NUMBER
```

Figure 2.5 – *Describe v$session_event*

The structure is very similar to *v$system_event*. However, there are two new fields in this view, SID and MAX_WAIT.

SID is the Session Identifier that allows establishment of a connection between the current session and a username by joining with the *v$session* view. This makes it easier to track down users since the username is what users log in with and generally they are not aware of their SID. In Oracle releases 9.2.0.1 and 9.2.0.2 the SID values are incorrect in this view. Metalink Note: 208105.1 provides information on this issue. Hence, any joins between *v$session_event* and *v$session* will return information for the wrong session unless *v$session.sid* - 1 is used in a join predicate. Testing confirms that this is fixed in 9.2.0.3.

MAX_WAIT is the maximum time in hundredths of a second that this event has been waited for by this session. If a particular user calls and reports that their session is intermittently "hanging," this may be a useful field. Being able to see this user's statistics for MAX_WAIT and AVERAGE_WAIT and compare them to others who are not experiencing the same delays provides valuable diagnostic information.

v$session_event allows the ability to dig into a specific session to see if the waits are common to other sessions. The following is an example situation where a user calls to say that the report they are running appears to be hung and they want to know what is going on.

Facts:
Name: Roger Smith
Username: SMITHRO
Logged in: This morning
Job Details: Weekly report usually runs in a few minutes, but today has not finished in an hour.

First get the users SID from *v$session* which can be done using *session_identification.sql*.

🖫 session_identification.sql

```
-- ***************************************************
-- Copyright © 2003 by Rampant TechPress
-- This script is free for non-commercial purposes
-- with no warranties.  Use at your own risk.
--
-- To license this script for a commercial purpose,
-- contact info@rampant.cc
-- ***************************************************

/* session_identification.sql */
col USERNAME Form a10
col SID form 99999
select
   SID,
```

```
   USERNAME,
   LOGON_TIME,
   STATUS
from
   V$SESSION
where
   USERNAME like UPPER('%&username%');
```

```
   SID USERNAME    LOGON_TIM STATUS
------ ----------- --------- --------
    14 SMITHRO     01-NOV-03 ACTIVE
   190 SMITHRO     19-NOV-03 INACTIVE
```

Figure 2.6 – SID Identification

Next, look at the *v$session_event* view, using this *session_events.sql* script:

🖫 session_events.sql

```
-- *************************************************
-- Copyright © 2003 by Rampant TechPress
-- This script is free for non-commercial purposes
-- with no warranties.  Use at your own risk.
--
-- To license this script for a commercial purpose,
-- contact info@rampant.cc
-- *************************************************

/* session_events.sql */
column SID            format 9999
column TOTAL_WAITS    format 999999 heading TOT|WAIT
column AVERAGE_WAIT   format 99999  heading AVG|WAIT
column EVENT          format a30

select
   SID,
   EVENT,
   TOTAL_WAITS,
   TIME_WAITED,
   AVERAGE_WAIT,
   MAX_WAIT
from
   V$SESSION_EVENT
where
   SID in (&sid_list) -- sid list generated from above query
order by
   TOTAL_WAITS;
```

```
                         TOT              AVG
  SID EVENT             WAIT TIME_WAITED  WAIT   MAX_WAIT
----- -------------- ------- ----------- ------- ----------
  190 enqueue          29349      27805        1          2
```

Figure 2.7 – Identification of wait events by SID

After running the previous query multiple times, notice that the enqueue event is increasing for the older session. Further research indicates that an enqueue wait is used for locking. After looking at blocking locks, it is determined that Roger himself, as shown in the other session listed above, is holding the lock that is preventing today's report from running. The user, Roger, indicates that it is safe to kill the older session. As soon as the older session is terminated, the user advises that the report just finished. After discussing this situation with the person that wrote this report, it is discovered that this report creates a staging table. Rogers' session from several days ago was holding a lock on this table and preventing today's report from completing.

Although *v$session_event* provided more specific information, sometimes more real-time information is needed. Use *v$session_wait* to meet that need.

v$session_wait

This view provides information about the current wait status of each session and gets updated by the log writer process every three seconds.

```
SQL> desc v$session_wait
 Name                            Null?      Type
 ------------------------------- ---------- -----------------
 SID                                        NUMBER
 SEQ#                                       NUMBER
 EVENT                                      VARCHAR2(64)
 P1TEXT                                     VARCHAR2(64)
 P1                                         NUMBER
 P1RAW                                      RAW(4)
 P2TEXT                                     VARCHAR2(64)
 P2                                         NUMBER
 P2RAW                                      RAW(4)
 P3TEXT                                     VARCHAR2(64)
 P3                                         NUMBER
 P3RAW                                      RAW(4)
 WAIT_TIME                                  NUMBER
 SECONDS_IN_WAIT                            NUMBER
 STATE                                      VARCHAR2(19)
```

Figure 2.7 – *Describe v$session_wait*

Until it is understood a little better, this may seem by far to be the most cryptic and confusing view of the three presented. It seems to be a complicated view for Oracle as well, given that there are a number of bugs associated with it. Be sure to research any bugs noted here to determine their potential impact.

Shortly after upgrading a database to 9i, it was noted while was investigating a slowness complaint that there were a large number of null events appearing in these views. Null events in this case were not the "idle" events mentioned earlier, but were events that had the name "null event." This was not very useful in diagnosing the performance problem. A quick search on Metalink revealed entries in the technical forums about a Bug 1743159, which is apparently not viewable on Metalink. The Note states: "A number of wait events use "null event" rather than distinct event names. With this fix a number of possible waits get proper event names." This bug is closed by development by stating that the problem is partially fixed in patchset 9.2.0.3 and completely in patchset 9.2.0.4 and version 10i.

The more important fields to note are:

- P1TEXT. Description of first wait-event parameter (P1).

- P1. Value of the first wait-event parameter in decimal.

- P2TEXT. Description of second wait-event parameter (P2)

- P2. Value of the second wait-event parameter in decimal.

- P3TEXT. Description of third wait-event parameter (P3)

- P3. Value of the third wait-event parameter in decimal.

- WAIT_TIME. If the value is zero (0), then the session is currently waiting. (Except for Bug # 2117360 on 9.0). If the value is −1, the duration of the last wait is less than 1/100th of a second in duration (less than 1 centisecond).

- SECONDS_IN_WAIT. This is the number of seconds between the current time and the time this event started when the WAIT_TIME is equal to 0 (i.e. when the session is waiting).

- STATE. Represents the current state of this wait or status. It can be one of the following values:

- WAITING means the session is currently waiting for a resource.

  o WAITED UNKNOWN TIME means the duration of last wait is unknown, but it is done waiting.

  o WAITED SHORT TIME means the last wait <1/100th of a second

  o WAITED KNOWN TIME means the value of WAIT_TIME is equal to the duration of last wait.

The RAW fields are simply the hexadecimal equivalent of the corresponding decimal field.

By using this view in a situation where waits continually occur for SQL*Net messages where WAIT_TIME is 0 in *v$session_wait*, it may be determined that network problems are the culprit. This is in spite of abundant documentation on Metalink and other places stating that these are idle waits.

A sample use of this query is shown using the *session_waits.sql* script.

🖫 session_waits.sql

```
--  ****************************************************
--  Copyright © 2003 by Rampant TechPress
--  This script is free for non-commercial purposes
--  with no warranties.  Use at your own risk.
--
--  To license this script for a commercial purpose,
--  contact info@rampant.cc
--  ****************************************************

/* session_waits.sql */
column event            format a20
column p1text           format a20
column p3text           format a8
column p2text           format a8
column seconds_in_wait  format 99999 heading SECONDS|IN_WAIT
column wait_time        format 999 heading WAIT|TIME
column state            format a20
column p1               format 999999
column p2               format 99
column p3               format 99

select
   SID,
   EVENT,
   P1TEXT,
   P1,
   P2TEXT,
   P2,
   P3TEXT,
   P3,
   WAIT_TIME,
   SECONDS_IN_WAIT,
   STATE
from
   V$SESSION_WAIT
order by
   EVENT;
```

```
WAIT SECONDS
SID EVENT                    P1TEXT    P1 P2TEXT  P2 P3TEXT P3 TIME IN_WAIT STATE
--- ---------------------- -------- ---- ------ --- ------ -- ---- ------- ----------------
  9 db file sequential read file#      43 block# 101 locks  1    0       0 WAITED KNOWN TIME
  1 pmon timer              duration 300         0           0    0       3 WAITING
  2 rdbms ipc message       timeout  300         0           0    0       0 WAITING
```

Figure 2.9 – Session Waits

That covers the basics of the "big three" views of the wait interface. There are other useful views that help dig into specific performance issues that will be covered briefly in the next sections.

v$event_name

Another view that is an important part of the Wait Interface is *v$event_name*. *v$evnet_name* is the roadmap and reference table that can be used anytime while exploring *v$session_wait*. It contains information about the wait events and what the P1, P2 and P3 values represent for each. In version 8.1.6, there are 212 events. In 9.2.0.1, there are 363 events. 9.2.0.2 has 369 and 9.2.0.3 is up to 399. This was tested on a variety of Linux, Tru64 and AIX operating systems with consistent results.

```
SQL>  desc v$event_name
 Name                     Null?       Type
 ---------------------- ----------  ---------------
 EVENT#                               NUMBER
 NAME                                 VARCHAR2(64)
 PARAMETER1                           VARCHAR2(64)
 PARAMETER2                           VARCHAR2(64)
 PARAMETER3                           VARCHAR2(64)
```

Figure 2.10 – *Describe v$event_name*

To demonstrate how this information can be used, the query *event_list.sql* retrieves data for wait events with a particular name. Figure 2.11 shows the output of that query when run using the phrase "db file."

```
-- *************************************************
-- Copyright © 2003 by Rampant TechPress
-- This script is free for non-commercial purposes
-- with no warranties.  Use at your own risk.
--
-- To license this script for a commercial purpose,
-- contact info@rampant.cc
-- *************************************************

/* event_list.sql */
column NAME format a25
select
    *
from
    V$EVENT_NAME
where
    NAME like '%&partial_event_name%';
```

```
EVENT# NAME                     PARAMETER1 PARAMETER2 PARAMETER3
------ ---------------------- ---------- ---------- ----------
   202 DFS db file lock         file#
   204 db file sequential read  file#      block#     blocks
   205 db file scattered read   file#      block#     blocks
   206 db file single write     file#      block#     blocks
   207 db file parallel write   requests   interrupt  timeout
   208 db file parallel read    files      blocks     requests
```

Figure 2.11 – Event List

When working with the *v$session_wait* view and viewing db file scattered read waits, it is now possible to determine that the value in P1 represents the file#.   And it is possible to use the *dba_data_files* data dictionary view to determine the file name and location. P2 in *v$session* represents the specific block# being read. By using *dba_extents*, it is possible to identify the specific object being read. If the object being read is partitioned, it is possible to see which partition is being read. Examples will be presented later.

v$filestat

One area that can surface as a problem area for performance is that of I/O operations. This view tracks the time it takes in milliseconds (ms) to complete I/O requests for the last, the worst, and the best operations as well as an average. It also keeps track of how many reads, writes, and how many blocks for each file. It is important to note that the times in the WRITETIM column are often incorrect. If the average write time (WRITETIM/PHYWRTS) looks nonsense then it probably is. Incorrect values typically show up as about 10 times more than one would expect. This information is from the Metalink support page, although it is not known if there is an official bug documenting the problem.

```
SQL> desc v$filestat
 Name                      Null?      Type
 ------------------------- ---------- -----------
 FILE#                                NUMBER
 PHYRDS                               NUMBER
 PHYWRTS                              NUMBER
 PHYBLKRD                             NUMBER
 PHYBLKWRT                            NUMBER
 SINGLEBLKRDS                         NUMBER
 READTIM                              NUMBER
 WRITETIM                             NUMBER
 SINGLEBLKRDTIM                       NUMBER
 AVGIOTIM                             NUMBER
 LSTIOTIM                             NUMBER
 MINIOTIM                             NUMBER
 MAXIORTM                             NUMBER
 MAXIOWTM                             NUMBER
```

Figure 2.12 – *Describe v$filestat*

v$tempstat

Here is a describe of the *v$tempstat* view.

```
SQL> desc v$tempstat
 Name                        Null?        Type
 ---------------------------  ----------  -----------
 FILE#                                    NUMBER
 PHYRDS                                   NUMBER
 PHYWRTS                                  NUMBER
 PHYBLKRD                                 NUMBER
 PHYBLKWRT                                NUMBER
 SINGLEBLKRDS                             NUMBER
 READTIM                                  NUMBER
 WRITETIM                                 NUMBER
 SINGLEBLKRDTIM                           NUMBER
 AVGIOTIM                                 NUMBER
 LSTIOTIM                                 NUMBER
 MINIOTIM                                 NUMBER
 MAXIORTM                                 NUMBER
 MAXIOWTM                                 NUMBER
```

Figure 2.13 – *Describe v$tempstat*

Notice that the structure of *v$tempstat* is the same as *v$filestat*. The significant difference is that *v$tempstat* contains information for temporary files. Just as a reminder, temporary tablespaces are used for certain operations, for example, sorts that are too big for memory for example can use temporary files. This use of temporary tables, although slower than a memory only operation, is faster than if the information was stored in a permanent tablespace. The use of permanent tablespaces would incur additional performance-impacting overhead due to recoverability requirements.

v$waitstat

Here is a describe of the *v$waitstat* view:

```
SQL> desc v$waitstat
 Name                        Null?        Type
 ---------------------------  ----------  ---------------
 CLASS                                    VARCHAR2(18)
 COUNT                                    NUMBER
 TIME                                     NUMBER
```

Figure 2.14 – *Describe v$waitstat*

This view lists block contention statistics for each class of data block. It is possible to view when block movement in and out of the buffer cache is causing slowness in the database with this view. If buffer cache problems are indicated by the other components of the wait interface this will provide, on a system-wide scope, what the waits are all about. The advantage is the ability to start tuning the buffer cache ratio here rather than when a low buffer cache hit-ratio is seen. Figure 2.15 shows the output that can be obtained by running *block_waits.sql*.

🖫 block_waits.sql

```
--  *********************************************
--  Copyright © 2003 by Rampant TechPress
--  This script is free for non-commercial purposes
--  with no warranties.  Use at your own risk.
--
--  To license this script for a commercial purpose,
--  contact info@rampant.cc
--  *********************************************

/* block_waits.sql */
select
    *
from
    V$WAITSTAT
where rownum < 11
order by
    TIME desc,
    COUNT desc;
```

CLASS	COUNT	TIME
data block	2644	11813
1st level bmb	36	806
segment header	12	28
sort block	0	0
free list	0	0
3rd level bmb	0	0
2nd level bmb	0	0
extent map	0	0
save undo header	0	0
save undo block	0	0

10 rows selected

Figure 2.15 – *Top 10 Classes of Block Contention*

This shows a "top ten" list of the largest classes of block contention. This information would be helpful if it is already determined that block contention is being experienced.

STATSPACK

In addition to using these views and scripts, it is possible to use STATSPACK to gather much, if not all, of the same information. STATSPACK has advantages such as built in snapshot statistics gathering instead of the process shown earlier. It also has a ready-made query in the form of a report called *spreport.sql* which can be found in most $ORACLE_HOME/rdbms/admin directories. The install is pretty straightforward, and it must be done before any data can be retrieved using it. This could be a definite disadvantage in a reactive performance tuning situation where a solution is needed NOW. Another problem could be that the report it produces is rather general in nature. While using tools like oraperf.com can help navigate this report, nothing beats a simple query that tells where a given session is waiting when the user is asking why this report is taking so long. That will be examined more with the use of STATSPACK in Chapter 7.

Benefits

In order to wrap up the discussion of the Wait Interface, it is important to highlight the benefits of using it instead of, or in addition to, other tuning methodologies. The nature of the Wait Interface makes analysis more precise than ratios. The analysis shows the specific area of concern, which allows for a more direct resolution. Whereas ratios take details of the activity of the database and summarize them into a single metric, the Wait Interface uses the details to let the DBA see what is slowing the database down. Ratios have a "one-trick pony" solution – the typical solution to a bad ratio is to throw more memory at the problem, which doesn't always work. The Wait Interface simply provides more accurate information, which *may* lead to adding more memory if warranted, but could lead elsewhere.

"I wonder if our processor is what is slowing down the database."

The Wait Interface measures where the database is spending its time waiting. This allows the DBA to focus efforts on areas that are currently acting as constraints or bottlenecks. This focusing of effort allows tuning activities to be more productive and efficient.

Another benefit of using the Wait Interface is that it allows the gathering of reliable performance numbers that can be used to establish "normal" service level for things like I/O operations. When troubleshooting problems, it is possible to know whether or not the current I/O performance is better/worse/comparable to what has been experienced under "normal" circumstances. This information will help when working with other areas like system administration or network administration to demonstrate that there is a problem with one of those components.

Limitations

One of the limitations of the Wait Interface is that the scope of the data in some of the views that make up the Wait Interface is too broad. If the scope of this data is not narrowed appropriately, there is a risk of misinterpreting the results resulting in trying to tune the wrong thing. For example, the *v$system_event* view contains data from the entire time that the instance has been running. This obscures current problems and makes it necessary to monitor changes rather than just the values. This is a bit more work and so is listed here as a limitation. Being aware of the limitations, allows the DBA to compensate with strategies like building temporary tables and calculating the difference between start and finish time periods that would provide the information need.

One possibility for overcoming this limitation of "too much data" would be to summarize the data from *v$session_event*. This would certainly eliminate much of the older data that is accumulated in *v$system_event*. That process does not eliminate some of the older data, since with some systems, it is common to see sessions logged in for several days at a time. This would be somewhat more accurate than querying *v$system_event* directly and easier than building start and stop tables. *v$session_event* only gets rid of data upon exit of the session so there could be data that is of no concerned.

In the author's opinion, another limitation is the opposite of the prior limitation in that some of the data has very short duration. In order to detect a problem when using *v$session_wait*, constant vigilance is required. When a user reports that their session is running slow and the pertinent information hasn't been gathered before their job finishes, it will be necessary to ask the user to re-run the problem report or job so that it can be monitored as it is running.

It is important to realize that *v$session_wait* only gets updated every 3 seconds. Considering how many operations get executed in a second with today's processors, it is plain to see that this view only shows a sample of the events that take place. This is not a problem most of the time. However, it is important to be aware of it as unusual results warrant further review. This is usually only an issue when there are a large number of wait events that are of a duration that does not regularly span the 3-second mark. When the short duration events are not the pre-dominant ones, this limitation does not cause a problem, since the longer waits are the ones causing problems and they show up clearly.

Another limitation is that when tuning a specific session or job, it is necessary to use some type of methodology to gather data for the session in question. That can be done with a shell script, Perl or Korn for example. A PL/SQL procedure or SQL scripts like some of the one demonstrated in this chapter are also useful. This is a limitation depending on DBA skills, since the DBA may not be as proficient in programming PL/SQL as in Perl. By limiting choice of scripting tools, the information gathering process could be more labor intensive than necessary.

Conclusion

In order to effectively use data from the Wait Interface for tuning activities, a way to save that data is required. In Orlando at IOUG Live! 2003, Richmond Shee in his presentation titled <u>10046 Alternatives</u> does a great job of highlighting several different ways to capture and use data from the Wait Interface. It is available to IOUG members in the Technical Repository and is recommended reading as it contains very good ideas on different options for gathering this data and explaining the advantages and disadvantages of each.

This chapter introduced one way to use Wait Analysis of the Wait Interface to determine where problems lie in database performance. The core of the Wait Interface are the three (3) views, *v$system_event, v$session_event and v$session_wait*. Examples were provided for ways to query these views to begin determining why users are calling saying "the database is slow!" Starting with chapter 5, more detail will be provided into how to apply these concepts in a meaningful way with real-life examples. Next Chapter 3 will introduce another way to use the wait information from the database by way of the 10046 Trace.

10046 Tracing – A Speed-Based Measurement System

Introduction

In the first two chapters, two different approaches to database tuning were covered. They were ratios and the wait interface. The wait interface was shown to be a better approach for most performance tuning.

Chapter 2 covered the wait interface's core structure, which predominantly uses the following views: *v$system_event*, *v$session_event* and *v$session_wait*. By using these structures provides great insight into the wait interface, but there are limitations and challenges that make data gathering difficult at times.

This chapter will cover the option of gathering data about where a process is spending its time by activating extended SQL tracing. This is accomplished by setting a specific event; either for a session or for the whole instance. Specifically, the process of how to set these events will be covered. Keep in mind that while it is possible to set events at the instance level, it may not always be a good idea. The reason being that events typically generate a large amount of data and will most likely fill up the mount point where trace data is being written. Also, the additional overhead incurred by setting events could negatively impact system performance.

Event Defined

In Metalink Note 121491.1, Oracle documentation defines an event as:

"A special item used by the Oracle server to do one of the following:

Change behavior

Enable collection of trace or debug information

Enable additional error checking or similar"

"Is this the sort of event that requires a caterer?"

Events are troubleshooting tools that copy important information to files for later analysis. This chapter focuses on the

---

10046 event. This event gathers information about the SQL that is executing, and enables the analysis of what is being done and what resources are being consumed. This provides insight into how to make the biggest impact on the performance of the specific session that was being traced.

Setting Events

Setting an event is telling the Oracle software that when it performs some function such as an event, it should not only perform the function, but should also document what actions it is taking.

This can be set at the instance level for all sessions that connect to a specific instance, although this is not advisable. There are many reasons to avoid setting an event or enabling SQL tracing for an entire instance. Some reasons noted are as follows:

- The large number of files that would be created can fill up the file system being used for storing this data.

- The extra burden tracing places on the system would likely be detrimental to the performance that users experience. Since, the reason for tracing is to fix a performance problem, making it worse is not a good idea.

It can also be set at a session level, either by the session user or by an administration-level user. This is considered a more favorable option.

Note: Oracle bug 2329767 states that tracing the PMON process can cause the instance to crash. The bug note states that it will be fixed in Oracle 10.0. So prior to upgrading and testing Oracle 10.0, do not trace PMON.

The basic principals of setting events to obtain SQL trace data will be introduced in this chapter. The mechanics will be explored and demonstrated more completely in Chapter 6 with the use of case studies focusing on using event 10046 to diagnose performance problems.

Event 10046

There are many events that have been built into the Oracle code. For example, when event 10408 is enabled, it blocks certain keywords as well as some built-in SQL functions that were added in version 8.1.6. When event 10053 is set, it enables the CBO (Cost Based Optimizer) trace. This trace allows the DBA to see on what Oracle based its choice for selecting a certain execution plan. Event 10066 will simulate a failure to verify a file.

There are many other events that can cause system instability or corruption. So, it is recommended that user not utilize them except under direction of their IT support staff. Event 10046 has been sufficiently documented so that, other than the risks already mentioned, there is little to no chance of anything occurring other than discovering what is making the system slow so it can be fixed.

Metalink Note 39817.1 reviews how to interpret the trace file that results from using event 10046. This chapter will cover some of the same information in this note. This is a fairly time consuming and difficult task, and it may be prudent to use other tools to help with this task. Some of these tools are discussed in the section on resources later in this chapter.

Prerequisites to Collecting SQL Trace Data

There are a couple prerequisite parameters that must be addressed no matter which method is used for enabling tracing. Timed statistics must be enabled in order to get timing information about the process. Timed statistics can be enabled at startup using the *pfile* or *spfile*. In the *pfile*, set the parameter to *timed_statistics* = TRUE, while the *spfile* could be updated with the following command:

```
ALTER SYSTEM SET TIMED_STATISTICS = TRUE SCOPE=BOTH;
```

In the early days of Oracle, possibly as recently as version 7, using this parameter had a negative impact, reportedly around 10%, on database performance. However, since version 8 and definitely in 9i and 10g, if there is any performance impact, it is widely believed to not be measurable.

In spite of this, Metalink documentation still appears to be divided on this issue. The reference note for this parameter states, "Normally, timed_statistics should be false." Meanwhile note 30824.1, states that the small amount of overhead from tuning this tracing on is worth the benefits gained.

In the face of this ambiguity from Oracle, many DBAs choose to leave this to *TRUE* on an instance-wide level for most databases. The exception to this is when a bug is impacting normal operations and cannot be patched.

It can also be enabled with either an ALTER SYSTEM or ALTER SESSION call at any time for either a specific session or the whole instance. There are a few ways to accomplish this, but only two ways are shown here. These should work for most installations.

For the current session:

```
alter session set timed_statistics = TRUE;
```

For a different session with Session IDentifier SID and Serial Number of SERIAL#:

```
exec sys.dbms_system.set_bool_param_in_session( SID, SERIAL#,
'timed_statistics', TRUE);
```

Another important thing to remember before tracing is that the trace dump file needs to be able to grow large enough so no important information is missed or the trace files will not be helpful. It is important to consider whether the ease of setting the *max_dump_file_size* once at the instance level is worth the risk of the destination getting full. For safety's sake, it is probably better to keep this small, 100k or so, for the production database's initialization parameter and then manually setting it to unlimited for specific sessions. Just remember to set it, or the trace files will not be helpful for tuning.

There are several ways to set this parameter. The focus here is to establish a reasonable value system-wide and a large value only for an individual session. Two ways that should accomplish this for most systems are covered here.

For the current session:

```
alter session set max_dump_file_size = UNLIMITED;
```

For a different session with Session IDentifier SID and Serial Number of SERIAL#:

```
exec sys.dbms_system.set_int_param_in_session( SID, SERIAL#,
'max_dump_file_size', 2000000000);
```

One optional parameter that could be helpful is *tracefile_identifier*. Using this parameter and setting it to the value specified in *unique_name* allows for easier identification of the specific trace file. Here is the syntax.

```
ALTER SESSION SET TRACEFILE_IDENTIFIER = 'unique_name';
```

To make these prerequisites simpler, there are two scripts in the code depot. The *prepare_other_session.sql* script will prompt for the *SID* and *SERIAL#*, and make these two changes to the session named. The *prepare_current_session.sql* script will make these two changes for the current session. Note: ALTER SESSION privilege is needed for these scripts to work.

🖫 prepare_other_session.sql

```
-- ****************************************************
-- Copyright © 2003 by Rampant TechPress
-- This script is free for non-commercial purposes
-- with no warranties.  Use at your own risk.
--
-- To license this script for a commercial purpose,
-- contact info@rampant.cc
-- ****************************************************

/* prepare_other_session.sql */
-- This script will make sure timed statistics
--     and max_dump_file_size are set correctly in
--     preparation for tracing a specific session.
accept SID prompt 'Enter the SID: '
accept SERIAL prompt 'Enter the SERIAL#: '

exec sys.dbms_system.set_bool_param_in_session( &SID, &SERIAL,
'timed_statistics', TRUE);
exec sys.dbms_system.set_int_param_in_session( &SID, &SERIAL,
'max_dump_file_size', 2000000000);
```

🖫 prepare_current_session.sql

```
-- ****************************************************
-- Copyright © 2003 by Rampant TechPress
-- This script is free for non-commercial purposes
-- with no warranties.  Use at your own risk.
--
-- To license this script for a commercial purpose,
```

```
-- contact info@rampant.cc
-- ****************************************************

/* prepare_current_session.sql */
-- This script will make sure timed statistics
--    and max_dump_file_size are set correctly
--    in the current session in preparation
--    for tracing.
alter session set max_dump_file_size = UNLIMITED;
alter session set timed_statistics = TRUE;
```

Levels

Before explaining more about the various ways to trace, a note about *levels* is called for. When tracing SQL statements, different levels of detail of the data can be gathered. Table 3.1 shows the specific levels available for SQL tracing.

LEVEL	INFORMATION GATHERED
0	None
1	Standard
4	Standard + bind values
8	Standard + wait information
12	Standard + binds + wait information

Table 3.1 – *Available Levels for Tracing*

Keep in mind that if Oracle's Wait Interface will be used to tune application code, either level 8 or level 12 must be used.

Collecting SQL Trace Data in Current Session

There are a number of ways to collect SQL trace data for the current session including *dbms_support* and ALTER SESSION SET EVENT. This next section will explain further.

An important part of tracing is that of *scope definition*. If the 'work part' of the process that was running is known, and the trace was started before or stopped after; then manually adjust for the time when the process was waiting for user input. This is important, because examining a trace file needs to be done correctly or the results of the analysis will be skewed, probably to the point of invalidating the research. If the measurement error can be measured, it may be possible to extract valid results from the file. However, it is easier and more accurate to start and stop the tracing activities accurately.

It may help to visualize it this way; at a NASCAR car race, the race stopwatch starts when the green flag is waved, and stops when the checkered flag is waved. That is the official duration of the race. If the stopwatch were started when the cars were on the warm-up lap before the race, or not stopped until after the celebration, there would not be an easy or accurate way to measure how long the race actually lasted. Because this is an area that is vital to getting accurate results, it is important that the best method for the situation be implemented.

With an in-house development group, it is possible to have the application changed to start gathering tracing information immediately before the job starts, and stop as soon as it is finished. This would provide fairly accurate results. With a third party application and no access to the code, it may be necessary to work cooperatively with the users to start and stop tracing for problematic jobs. Another alternative is to implement a trigger based solution.

Since the end result of tracing is essentially the same, differing only in the level of data that is collected, space will be conserved by only showing portions of one sample trace file at the end of this section.

Other ways to trace include:

- ORADEBUG (Oracle 7.3 and later)
- ORADBX (Before Oracle 7.3)
- ALTER SESSION SET SQL_TRACE

There are also third party applications such as Sparky (from HOTSOS.com) and Oracle's own Enterprise Manager, which offer the ability to trace specific sessions. Other alternatives can be researched through Metalink or other vendors.

What's in a name?

Pay close attention to the names of both the packages and procedures. *set_sql_trace_in_session* is very similar to *start_trace_in_session* and *dbms_support* is very close to *dbms_system*. If the two are mixed up, in the best case an error message will be generated. In the worst case, unexpected output will likely be the result. *set_sql_trace_in_session* only provides level 1 data. That is a problem when looking for information on waits and bind variables.

ALTER SESSION SET EVENTS

This is a simple command that is similar in structure and syntax to one DBAs have used for years. The *ALTER SESSION* command is very versatile and familiar. The syntax used for this command to enable tracing for the current session is simply:

```
ALTER SESSION SET EVENTS '10046 trace name context forever, level 12';
```

This creates a file in the directory defined by the *user_dump_dest* parameter. There are several reasons why identifying the trace file can be challenging. One reason is that the *user_dump_dest* is defined at the database level, so it is necessary to check the setting for the database being traced. The other reason is that the name of a trace file is inconsistent across different platforms. For example, for a 9.2.0.3 database on Linux (RedHat 7.3) with a database *oracle_sid* set to toy, the file is named *toy_ora_16409.trc*. 16409 is the operating system process id (spid) of the process being traced. For an 8.1.6.1 database named test, the trace file is named *ora_16511.trc* where 16511 is the spid.

The same tests in both HP Tru64 and IBM AIX produce the same name patterns involving some combination of the operating system process identifier, the database name, and the letters ora. For other operating systems, this is really only difficult the first time until the particular naming pattern for the environment is learned. This is also simplified by another available setting mentioned earlier in this chapter, *tracefile_identifier*, which will include the phrase *find_me* in the file name of the trace file. Intelligent use of this option makes identification of trace files easier. For example, if tracing in response to a help desk problem report, the ticket or case number might be included here. This feature was introduced in 8.1.7 and cannot be done for background processes.

To stop tracing, it is simpler still:

```
ALTER SESSION SET EVENTS '10046 trace name context off';
```

This is pretty easy, but exiting the program may be an easier solution. Exiting the session normally (exit from SQL*Plus for example) causes additional information to be written that captures the explain plan in the trace file. This will not work for three-tier applications, as the sessions are persistent across multiple user connections. It will be necessary to use the ALTER SESSION SET EVENTS command in these instances to turn tracing off to avoid a huge trace file that is not properly scoped.

DBMS_SUPPORT.START_TRACE ()

Besides the *ALTER SESSION* command, the *dbms_support* package provides a procedure called *start_trace*. This procedure accepts two parameters both of which are Boolean values. If the first is *TRUE*, information on *WAIT* is collected, and if the second is *TRUE*, information on *BIND* values is collected. Figure 3.2 is an expanded version of Figure 3.1 showing the various Level settings.

Level	Information Gathered	WAITS	BINDS
0	None	n/a (*)	n/a (*)
1	Standard	FALSE	FALSE
4	Standard + bind values	FALSE	TRUE
8	Standard + wait information	TRUE	FALSE
12	Standard + binds + wait information	TRUE	TRUE

(*) n/a This level of tracing is achieved with the STOP_TRACE procedures

Figure 3.2 – *dbms_support to trace level conversion*

Using this procedure is fairly simple. An example follows:

```
SQL> execute sys.dbms_support.start_trace (true,true);

PL/SQL procedure successfully completed.
```

One that is done, proceed to do the work that is being traced. After tracing is completed, either exit the session, or use the *stop_trace* procedure as follows:

```
SQL> execute sys.dbms_support.stop_trace;

PL/SQL procedure successfully completed.
```

Be aware that the *dbms_support* package is not always installed by default. However, it can be installed, by running *$ORACLE_HOME/rdbms/admin/dbmssupp.sql*.

A note about rights

Sometimes when trying to trace a session and the user is unable to start tracing, it is probably just a rights issue. This can be fixed by granting the user execute privileges on this package as demonstrated in the following example.

```
SQL> conn kevin/kevin
Connected.
SQL> execute sys.dbms_support.start_trace (true,true);
BEGIN sys.dbms_support.start_trace (true,true); END;
     *
ERROR at line 1:
ORA-06550: line 1, column 7:
PLS-00201: identifier 'SYS.DBMS_SUPPORT' must be declared
ORA-06550: line 1, column 7:
PL/SQL: Statement ignored

SQL> conn / as sysdba
Connected.
SQL> grant execute on dbms_support to kevin;

Grant succeeded.

SQL> conn kevin/kevin
Connected.
SQL>  execute sys.dbms_support.start_trace (true,true);

PL/SQL procedure successfully completed.
```

Collecting SQL Trace Data in Other Sessions

DBMS_SYSTEM.SET_EV()

This package contains several helpful procedures including:

- *set_int_param_in_session*
- *set_ev*

- *set_bool_param_in_session*

Earlier in this chapter examples of uses for the *set_int_param_in_session* procedure and the *set_bool_param_in_session* procedure were provided. Now the *set_ev* procedure and one way to use its functionality will be covered.

set_ev is short for SET EVent and it accepts five parameters. The first four will be explained here, and the fifth should be left set to a null field with two single quotes side-by-side with no space (''). The *dbms_system* package is officially unsupported by Oracle and the fifth field is undocumented and not intended to be used outside of Oracle.

The four remaining parameters are:

- *SID*

- *Serial#*

- *Event*

- *Level*

SID and *Serial#* are the identifiers that can be used to uniquely specify the particular session or process in the database that is of interest. Use the *session_identification.sql* script introduced in Chapter 2 to get these pieces of information.

Event should be set to the event number that will be traced. In this book, it will always be 10046. It is strongly advised not to set any other without good counsel and/or direction from Oracle Support.

Level is the detail that is desired. Use the table in Figure 3.1 to determine the setting for *Level*. All four of these parameters are numeric. Here is the output from using the *session_identification.sql* followed by executing this procedure to enable level 12 tracing for a user whose last name is ANDERT. In this example, ANDERT must be part of the userid:

```
SQL> @session_identification
Enter value for username: ANDERT
old  10:     USERNAME like UPPER('%&username%')
new  10:     USERNAME like UPPER('%ANDERT%')

   SID    SERIAL# USERNAME   LOGON_TIM STATUS
------ ---------- ---------- --------- --------
     8         45 ANDERTST   20-DEC-03 INACTIVE

SQL> execute dbms_system.set_ev (8, 45,10046,12,'');

PL/SQL procedure successfully completed.
```

If trouble is encountered executing this procedure, make sure the user executing it has direct grants from the owner (sys). Also ensure that either a public synonym has been created or the procedure is referred to with owner-prefixed notation.

DBMS_SUPPORT.START_TRACE_IN_SESSION()

This is the procedure that Oracle prefers be used to control tracing activities. Using this procedure removes the possibility of unintentionally typing the wrong event number. This procedure uses similar syntax to *dbms_support.start_trace*. The following command is used to enable level 12 tracing in the session identified by *sid* and *serial#*:

```
EXECUTE DBMS_SUPPORT.START_TRACE_IN_SESSION(sid, serial#,
waits=>TRUE, binds=>TRUE)
```

Refer back to Figure 3.2 to see how to determine what level is represented by any given combination of Boolean values for the *binds* and *waits* parameters.

Figure 3.3 is a sample run using several scripts to identify and prepare a given session for the final command to start tracing.

```
SQL>  @session_identification
Enter value for username: WEB

  SID    SERIAL# USERNAME   LOGON_TIM STATUS
------ ---------- ---------- --------- --------
   15       292 WEBBER     21-DEC-03 ACTIVE
   19       654 WEBBER     21-DEC-03 ACTIVE

SQL> @prepare_other_session
Enter the SID: 19
Enter the SERIAL#: 654

PL/SQL procedure successfully completed.

PL/SQL procedure successfully completed.

SQL> EXECUTE SYS.DBMS_SUPPORT.START_TRACE_IN_SESSION(19, 654, waits=>TRUE, binds=>TRUE);

PL/SQL procedure successfully completed.
```

Figure 3.3 – *Starting tracing in another session*

Examining a Trace File

At first glance, a trace file can be pretty intimidating. This section will provide some knowledge of a process just by examining a raw trace file. Like the rest of this book, rather than just theory, this section will focus on real trace files. The first file is named *toy_ora_32622_find_me.trc*. This trace file and the others that will be shown could be generated by any of the methods previously discussed in this chapter.

```
 1 /app/oracle/admin/TOY/udump/toy_ora_32622_find_me.trc
 2
 3 Oracle9i Enterprise Edition Release 9.2.0.3.0 - Production
 4 With the Partitioning, OLAP and Oracle Data Mining options
 5 JServer Release 9.2.0.3.0 - Production
 6 ORACLE_HOME = /app/oracle/product/9.2.0
 7 System name:    Linux
 8 Node name:      matthew
 9 Release:        2.4.18-3
10 Version:        #1 Thu Apr 18 07:31:07 EDT 2002
11 Machine:        i586
12 Instance name: TOY
13 Redo thread mounted by this instance: 1
14 Oracle process number: 9
15 Unix process pid: 32622, image: oracle@matthew (TNS V1-V3)
16
17 *** 2003-12-16 23:27:24.051
18 *** SESSION ID:(14.1906) 2003-12-16 23:27:24.049
19 APPNAME mod='SQL*Plus' mh=3669949024 act='' ah=4029777240
20 =====================
21 PARSING IN CURSOR #1 len=69 dep=0 uid=5 oct=42 lid=5
tim=1046525824269291 hv=1494869006 ad='5487450c'
22 ALTER SESSION SET EVENTS '10046 trace name context forever, level
12'
23 END OF STMT
24 EXEC
#1:c=0,e=31785,p=0,cr=0,cu=0,mis=1,r=0,dep=0,og=4,tim=10465258242672
59
25 WAIT #1: nam='SQL*Net message to client' ela= 16 p1=1650815232
p2=1 p3=0
26 WAIT #1: nam='SQL*Net message from client' ela= 2086543
p1=1650815232 p2=1 p3=0
```

Presented above are the first 26 lines of this trace file. This section will be used to explain what information is being reported. The goal here is not to cover every detail of a trace file, but to provide a reasonable guide to the trace file's structure, and to identify some key information that is available within. Further research is recommended and can be found on OTN and Metalink. Other options that exist for getting information out of trace files will be discussed in the resources section later in this chapter.

Line 1: This is simply the full path and file name of this trace file. Note - *find_me* is part of the file name, and comes from the *tracefile_identifier* session setting.

Lines 3-5: These lines contain version information that is important and helpful, especially for comparing processes that run better in one version than another. It is good to have this information handy if working with Oracle Support as they ask for specific version information.

Lines 6-13: These lines show information about the specific environment including the location of the Oracle Home that was used, the host server name, the operating system, and version.

Lines 14-15: These lines report the session specific information including the UNIX *pid* that the database session is using.

Lines 17-18: These lines report the date and time. Note - these times are reported down to milliseconds. On line 18, there is additional information about the current session, most notably, the SID and *SERIAL#*; 14 and 1906 in this file.

Line 19: The *dbms_application_info* is available to developers and allows them to set the module or action name. If it is used, this line will report that information; *mod* is the module name, *mh* is a hash value that represents the module name, *act* is the action name, and *ah* is the hash that represents the action name. In our example, the module name is 'SQL*Plus'. The action is set to a null string. The hash values are set according to something inside the database engine.

Lines 20-27: This is the information on the first cursor that was encountered after starting the trace and represents the core data that tracing is being done for. Therefore, these lines will be covered in more detail.

- **Line 21** – The phrase *PARSING IN CURSOR #1* describes cursor number 1. Among other information, the SQL statement in this cursor is 69 characters long (len=69) and is not a dependent cursor; i.e., not a child to another process.

- **Line 22** – This is the text of the SQL statement in the cursor.

- **Line 23** – The phrase *END OF STATEMENT* means that the end of the SQL statement in this cursor has been reached.

- **Line 24** – *EXEC* lines are information about the actual time spent by the cursor while executing. The value for C is the amount of CPU that was used during this operation, and the value of E is the elapsed time during this operation. In Oracle9i, these values are reported in microseconds. To tie this back in to the earlier commuting example; C is the time spent while the car is moving, and E is the total time from leaving home until arriving at work. E - C would represent the time the car was stopped at stoplights.

- **Lines 25-26** – *WAIT* lines provide information on the spent waiting for the cursor to get information from another source. The lines in the example, 'SQL*Net message...' are indicative of network latency. Other common events are 'db file sequential read' and 'db file scattered read'. They indicate that the process being traced was waiting for data that was not in the buffer cache and needed to be read from disk. *ela* is the total elapsed time of this event.

This is only an introduction to trace files. Although, it is not impossible to make sense out of the apparent gibberish, time must be spent learning about the syntax and rules. For a deeper understanding of 10046 trace files, read "Optimizing Oracle Performance" by Cary Millsap, which gives comprehensive coverage to this topic. The remainder of this chapter will cover ways to benefit from trace files, without having to understand more than has already been covered.

Resources

As mentioned previously, the output from a 10046 trace can be very large. Analyzing these files by hand can be very time-consuming and error-prone. Thankfully, there are some resources and tools that can ease this process.

Don't go ape trying to analyze 10046 trace files by hand.

While there may be others, the primary tools to be covered here are TKPROF and trace analyzer from Oracle, and Profiler from hotsos.com. Additionally, it is quite possible to use system utilities like *awk* and *grep* to perform some types of analysis. Perl also lends itself quite well to this type of analysis, and there may be an open source tool that has been developed to meet this need. The intention is not to endorse or recommend any particular solution, but to discuss the options that are available while providing information so the DBA can decide how to analyze the trace data to best meet their needs and the needs of the company or client.

TKPROF

TKPROF is a utility that Oracle provides to help make sense of raw trace files. It has been available for quite some time, at least back to version 7. It offers some benefits over manual analysis of trace files; most importantly, it is much easier to run TKPROF than to spend hours digging through a trace file. Another benefit is that it is included with Oracle database software and installed with the database so there is no additional cost to use it.

TKPROF is run like any other program with a couple parameters passed to tell it how to process the trace file. A brief example will be presented here. For further research into this utility, read the Oracle documentation, pick up one of many other books like Dave Moore's "Oracle Utilities", or read any of several articles like "Doc ID: 142898.1" from Metalink or other web sites to get a deeper understanding of the power of this tool.

A sample run of this tool using the trace file that was explained in the previous section looks like this:

```
$ tkprof toy_ora_32622_find_me.trc tkprof_32622.trc
explain=system/manager waits=y sort=PRSCNT
```

Executing the above command produces a file named tkprof_32622.trc. It includes an explain plan based on the user SYSTEM that will include a summary of the wait events found in the trace file. The SQL statements will be sorted based on the count of parses. The output file will look like Figure 3.4.

```
 1 TKPROF: Release 9.2.0.3.0 - Production on Wed Dec 17 22:23:21 2003
 2
 3 Copyright (c) 1982, 2002, Oracle Corporation.  All rights reserved.
 4
 5 Trace file: toy_ora_32622_find_me.trc
 6 Sort options: prscnt
 7 ********************************************************************************
 8 count    = number of times OCI procedure was executed
 9 cpu      = cpu time in seconds executing
10 elapsed  = elapsed time in seconds executing
11 disk     = number of physical reads of buffers from disk
12 query    = number of buffers gotten for consistent read
13 current  = number of buffers gotten in current mode (usually for update)
14 rows     = number of rows processed by the fetch or execute call
15 ********************************************************************************
16
17 select blocks,NVL(ts#,-1),status$,NVL(relfile#,0),maxextend,inc, crscnwrp,
18   crscnbas,NVL(spare1,0)
19 from
20  file$ where file#=:1
21
22
23 call       count       cpu     elapsed       disk      query     current        rows
24 -------   ------   --------  ----------  ---------  ---------  ----------  ----------
25 Parse         6      0.01        0.01          0          0           0           0
26 Execute       6      0.02        0.00          0          0           0           0
27 Fetch         6      0.00        0.00          0         12           0           6
28 -------   ------   --------  ----------  ---------  ---------  ----------  ----------
29 total        18      0.03        0.02          0         12           0           6
30
31 Misses in library cache during parse: 1
32 Optimizer goal: CHOOSE
33 Parsing user id: SYS    (recursive depth: 1)
34
35 Rows       Row Source Operation
36 -------    ---------------------------------------------------
37       1    TABLE ACCESS BY INDEX ROWID OBJ#(17) (cr=2 r=0 w=0 time=203 us)
38       1     INDEX UNIQUE SCAN OBJ#(41) (cr=1 r=0 w=0 time=91 us)(object id 41)
```

Figure 3.4 – *Sample TKPROF output*

The following is a line-by-line description of the output.

Lines 1-4: Version and execution date and time information.

Line 5: Trace file name.

Line 6: Sorts that were used to produce this output report. The count of parse calls in this example.

Lines 7-15: Additional information about the columns that are listed in the measurements section of the report.

Lines 17-20: Top SQL statement according to the sort specified when running TKPROF and reported on line 6.

Lines 23-29: Measurements section. Compare the number of parses and executes, one parse to many executes is good. All the information in this section is helpful to understand the work this SQL statement needs to do.

Lines 35-38: The explain plan used to execute this SQL statement. Notice that there is a field called time. This field reports the time taken for each step and its children steps. In this example, the time taken as shown on line 37 is about 200 microseconds.

There are many sort options that are available, especially with Oracle 9.2.x. Additional reading to learn more about this tool is recommended.

Trace Analyzer

Trace analyzer is an application from Oracle with much the same purpose as TKPROF. It is also designed to help analyze the trace files generated by SQL tracing. Trace analyzer offers enhancements over TKPROF in a number of areas. Several of the key improvements are discussed as follows:

- Trace Analyzer provides a more detailed list of wait events for every SQL statement that is part of the trace file. Whereas, only in recent versions has TKPROF provided at least limited wait information. Older versions provide no information on wait events regardless of the trace data.

- Trace Analyzer reports totals for statements that execute multiple times; whereas, TKPROF would report each execution separately. This is important when tracing a process that is updating many records, but doing it one row at a time. Identifying this with TKPROF, requires more manual effort.

- Trace Analyzer provides the values used by bind variables, as long as the trace file was generated at a level that includes bind variables; whereas, this feature is not available with TKPROF.

Trace Analyzer has other benefits that will be demonstrated in examples later this section as well as Chapter 6, in the Case Study section.

Installation of this can be a bit tricky. Unfortunately, this tool seems to be largely unknown or at least unused given the lack of hits when searching Metalink. Even the World Wide Web comes up with little information on using this tool and troubleshooting its installation. Metalink document 224270.1 provides an adequate explanation for finding the files to accomplish the installation as well as how to install and use it.

Another resource in addition to the Metalink document is on the Puget Sound Oracle User Group web page. There is a summary of steps that worked for Daniel Morgan who has shared his knowledge with the world. This document can be found at http://www.psoug.org/reference/trace_analyzer.html. Take a look at it if the Metalink document does provide adequate assistance when installing Trace Analyzer.

It seems that trying to install or use Trace Analyzer with a user account that does not have enough privileges causes most of the errors. Privileges need to be granted directly rather than through a role. This occurs mainly when attempting a select on some of the *dba_%* and *v$* views. Privileges which may normally be granted to a user with the DBA role would need to be direct grants in order for a user to create the procedures involved in the execution of Trace Analyzer.

These grants can be accomplished by running the *TRCA_grants.sql* script as the sys user. Notice that the naming style of this script is different from the rest of the scripts in this book. This script was named to fit with the Trace Analyzer scripts from Metalink. Therefore, it follows the naming standard of the TRCA prefix. A sample run is shown in Figure 3.5 with the additional confirmation messages omitted.

🖫 TRCA_grants.sql

```
--  ***************************************************
-- Copyright © 2003 by Rampant TechPress
-- This script is free for non-commercial purposes
-- with no warranties.  Use at your own risk.
--
-- To license this script for a commercial purpose,
-- contact info@rampant.cc
--  ***************************************************

/* This script will prompt for a username and
   then grant select privilege on all of the
   objects required for Trace Analyzer.  */
accept USER_NAME prompt 'Enter the username for TRCA: '

GRANT SELECT
   ON dba_indexes
   TO &USER_NAME;
GRANT SELECT
   ON dba_ind_columns
   TO &USER_NAME;
GRANT SELECT
   ON dba_objects
   TO &USER_NAME;
GRANT SELECT
   ON dba_tables
   TO &USER_NAME;
GRANT SELECT
   ON dba_temp_files
   TO &USER_NAME;
GRANT SELECT
   ON dba_users
   TO &USER_NAME;
GRANT SELECT
   ON v_$instance
   TO &USER_NAME;
GRANT SELECT
   ON v_$latchname
   TO &USER_NAME;
GRANT SELECT
   ON v_$parameter
   TO &USER_NAME;
```

```
SQL> @TRCA_grants
DOC>   then grant select privilege on all of the
DOC>   objects required for Trace Analyzer.   */
Enter the username for TRCA: SCOTT

Grant succeeded.
```

Figure 3.5 – *TRCA_grants sample run*

After successfully installing Trace Analyzer, it is simple to use in its basic form. Run the *TRCANLZR.sql;* with the first parameter *UDUMP,* for SQL trace files generated by users or user processes, and the trace file name as the second parameter. The installation instructions note that the case of these files is important. Use UPPERCASE name with lowercase extensions. This may be different from usual practice, but for the sake of sanity, it is best to leave it that way.

The output from running this script is stored in a log file named similar to the original trace file. It is prefixed with the word *TRCANLZR* and suffixed with *LOG* instead of trc. A portion of the results from our sample trace file is shown in the next two figures.

```
***************************************************************************************************;
TRCANLZR.sql 115.9  NOTE:224270.1  2003-12-16 19:45:57  Trace Analyzer
***************************************************************************************************;

TRACE_DIRECTORY..........: /app/oracle/admin/TOY/udump (ALIAS:UDUMP)
TRACE_FILENAME...........: TOY_ora_1530550_find_me.trc (TRACE_ID:1)
INCLUDE_SYS_COMMANDS.....: YES

INSTANCE_AND_RELEASE.... : TOY (ON MATTHEW)  9.2.0.2.0 (OSF1 - PRODUCTION)
TRACE_SIZE...............: 64518 BYTES (IN 1020 LINES)
TRACED_INTERVAL..........: STARTED ON 2003-12-16 19:41:29.572, AND LASTED 3.58 SECS

USER_ELAPSED_TIME........: 3.58 SECS
GAPS_WITH_NO_ACTIVITY....: 0.00
EFFECTIVE_TRACED_INTERVAL: 3.58

ACCOUNTED_CPU_TIME.......: 0.47 SECS (TOTAL SERVICE TIME)
ACCOUNTED_ELAPSED_TIME...: 1.78 (RECURSIVE AND NON-RECURSIVE)

WAITED_NON-IDLE_TIME.....: 0.33 SECS
WAITED_IDLE_TIME.........: 3.53


***************************************************************************************************;
NUMBER_OF_CURSORS........: 5 (USER),  23 (INTERNAL <SYS>),  28 (TOTAL)
UNIQUE_SQL...............: 3 (USER),  22 (INTERNAL <SYS>),  25 (TOTAL)

***************************************************************************************************;
TOP SQL (SUMMARY OF CPU, ELAPSED AND WAITS PER TOP EXPENSIVE CURSOR)
=================================================================

cursor user                                                      non-idle        idle
id     id   command type        count      cpu top   elapsed top  waits top    waits top
------ ---- ------------------- --------- --------- --- --------- --- --------- --- --------- ---
24.... 22.. select..............      9     0.38 1     1.25 1      0.02          0.05 2
10.... 0... select..............      6     0.02 2     0.14 2      0.01          0.00 4
2..... 22.. pl/sql execute......      6     0.02 3     0.02        0.00          3.48 1
6..... 0... select..............      4     0.02 4     0.04        0.03 4        0.00
25.... 0... select..............    248     0.02 5     0.01                      0.00
3..... 0... select..............     13     0.00        0.07 3      0.05 2        0.00
```

Figure 3.6 – *Trace Analyzer Summary and Header*

It is easy to see some of the differences between this output and the raw trace file. Some differences, like nice formatting of the header information shown in Figure 3.6, make it easier to read. The summary information, like the user elapsed time and accounted for CPU time (.47 seconds), provides a good overview picture of the trace interval.

This figure also identifies the top SQL statements ordered by CPU time, elapsed time, idle and non-idle waits by cursor. Notice that even though the select statement in cursor 25 has the most occurrences at 248, it is only the fifth worst statement in terms of CPU usage, and is not in the top five in all of the other categories.

Also notice that cursor 24 was only executed nine times, yet it is still the top cursor in terms of CPU and elapsed times, and close to the top in the idle waits category. Note - idle wait as a category defined by Oracle and the Trace Analyzer may not be the same one the DBA wishes to use.

Chapter 2 introduced the concept of idle waits and times when they may be very important to the tuning process. Chapter 5 will revisit this in more detail, but for now, knowing that Trace Analyzer provides the top SQL information by these other metrics, including waits, is the key point.

```
SUMMARY OF CALLS BY USER (INTERNAL LAST) AND NON-RECURSIVE/RECURSIVE
====================================================================

OVERALL TOTALS PER CALL FOR ALL NON-RECURSIVE STATEMENTS FOR USER 22 (ORADBA)

call        count      cpu   elapsed        disk        query      current          rows    misses
-------    -------  -------  --------   ---------   ----------  -----------    ----------  --------
Parse          4     0.07      0.42          48          116            0             0         2
Execute        5     0.02      0.02           0            0            0             3         1
Fetch          7     0.32      0.83           0         1291          245            29         0
-------    -------  -------  --------   ---------   ----------  -----------    ----------  --------
total         16     0.40      1.27          48                        245            32         3

OVERALL TOTALS PER CALL FOR ALL RECURSIVE STATEMENTS FOR INTERNAL USER 'SYS'

call        count      cpu   elapsed        disk        query      current          rows    misses
-------    -------  -------  --------   ---------   ----------  -----------    ----------  --------
Parse         23     0.05      0.16          15           28            0             0        22
Execute       34     0.02      0.04           0            3            0             0         0
Fetch        330     0.00      0.32          47          364            0           312         0
-------    -------  -------  --------   ---------   ----------  -----------    ----------  --------
total        387     0.07      0.51          62          395            0           312        22

**********************************************************************************************

SUMMARY OF CALLS BY COMMAND TYPE, USER (INTERNAL LAST) AND NON-RECURSIVE/RECURSIVE
=================================================================================

OVERALL TOTALS PER COMMAND TYPE FOR ALL NON-RECURSIVE STATEMENTS FOR USER 22 (ORADBA)

command type            count      cpu   elapsed       disk       query     current        rows   misses
-------------------   -------  -------  --------   --------  ----------  ----------   ---------  -------
select..............       9     0.38      1.25         48        1407         245          29        1
alter session.........     1     0.00      0.00          0           0           0           0        1
pl/sql execute.........    6     0.02      0.02          0           0           0           3        1
-------------------   -------  -------  --------   --------  ----------  ----------   ---------  -------
total.................    16     0.40      1.27         48        1407         245          32        3
```

Figure 3.7 – *Call Summary by User and Command Type*

Figure 3.7 displays the output provided by Trace Analyzer and reveals other information like total call counts with information about CPU, and disk and row counts by user. Note - the sum of the CPU times in this section of the report add up to .47 seconds which is the same as the CPU time in the first summary section.

This is incredibly valuable, since it would take a lot of work to gather and analyze the raw trace file to get that information. This indicates which commands and which part of the commands contributed most to the CPU and disk usage. This makes the Trace Analyzer very helpful when troubleshooting sticky performance problems.

Hotsos Profiler™

First, Profiler is not an Oracle Corp utility. Cary Millsap and Gary Goodman founded Hotsos.com when they saw a need for a performance problem-solving tool. Working with others, they developed Hotsos Profiler. This tool makes short work out of analyzing trace files. All that is needed is to upload a trace file to a web portal or use the available stand-alone tool. Then a report can be reviewed that contains summarized data to help identify the problem.

This tool overcomes some of the weaknesses in the other tools. Similar to Trace Analyzer, Hotsos Profiler makes the trace file summary and header information more presentable. See Figure 3.8. One of the things Hotsos Profiler adds is in the Interval Resource Profile that shows the Response Time Components. It makes it very clear which component, wait event or CPU time, was primarily responsible for the duration of this task. From there, clicking on the hyperlink navigates to the section of the report where the specific SQL Statement ID's can be found. They too are sorted in descending order by their contribution to the given response time component so it is easier to identify the most expensive statement. The SQL statement ID is also hyperlinked to the SQL statement summary. This provides specific information on the statement and will allow a competent person to resolve the bottleneck that is holding back performance.

```
       Oracle instance = CLAIM (9.2.0.2.0)
                  host = dgrdb01nl (OSF1 V5.1)
               program = oracle@dgrdb01nl(TNS V1-V3) (session 279)
            trace file = claim_ora_1373101.trc
            line count = 90 (0 ignored, 0 oracle error)
                    t0 = Fri Dec 12 2003 01:30:10 (449336619008)
                    t1 = Fri Dec 12 2003 01:31:37 (449424118008)
     interval duration = 87.499000s
          transactions = 1 (1 commit, 0 rollbacks)
              sessions = 1 (switches 0)
```

Interval Resource Profile

				-------------------- Duration Per Call --
Response Time Component	Duration		# Calls	Avg	Min
---	---	---	---	---	---
(i) SQL*Net message from client	92.171264s	105.3%	7	13.167323s	0.000000s
(i) CPU service	0.000000s	0.0%	15	0.000000s	0.000000s
(i) SQL*Net message to client	0.000000s	0.0%	7	0.000000s	0.000000s
(i) unaccounted-for	-4.672264s	-5.3%			
Total	87.499000s	100.0%			

Contribution to Response Time Component by SQL Statement

(i) SQL*Net message from client

				-------------------- Duration Per Call --
SQL Statement Id	Duration		# Calls	Avg	Min
---	---	---	---	---	---
3577214480	83.248128s	90.3%	3	27.749376s	0.001024s
3578532854	8.913920s	9.7%	3	2.971307s	0.000000s
1432236634	0.009216s	0.0%	1	0.009216s	0.009216s
Total	92.171264s	100.0%	7	13.167323s	0.000000s

Figure 3.8 – *Profiler sample screen*

The ease of use makes this a very good tool when analyzing a trace file. It is also very helpful when explaining to Developers why it is necessary to work with them on a particular SQL statement or help them to change a coding practice.

Benefits of 10046 Tracing

Collecting and analyzing the data that can be obtained by a 10046 trace provides specific information about the performance of a specific session. This is often more beneficial than looking at the *v$* information since much of that information can be from sessions that are not a key part of the performance problem, or can be from earlier in the users sessions and have no bearing on the current problem.

Limitations of 10046 Tracing

The Multi-Threaded Server (MTS) makes using this process more difficult. Use of application servers that establish "generic" connections to the database also limit the ease with which this tool can be used.

Conclusion

This chapter has introduced 10046 Tracing and the benefits that it brings to a tuning effort. The challenges to collecting and interpreting this information were discussed. Additionally, some of the resources available for facilitating this were introduced:

- TKPROF
- Trace Analyzer
- Hotsos Profiler

The next section of this book will go into more details on using Wait Event information in practical ways to efficiently tune Oracle databases.

The Importance of Holistic Tuning

Introduction

Merriam-Webster's online dictionary (http://www.m-w.com/cgi-bin/dictionary) defines holistic as "relating to or concerned with wholes or with complete systems rather than with the analysis of, treatment of, or dissection into parts." In other words, it is simply acknowledging that in the same way the human body has the 'elbow-bone connected to the shoulder bone,' database performance is tied to not only the database, but to the application server, the network, storage sub-system and many other factors. Due to this inter-connectivity, any tuning activities need to include a way to identify the source of the problem; even if it is not within the database itself. Then they need to determine what impact fixing that problem will have on the rest of the system.

*"There! Elbow-bone connected to the shoulder bone,
I knew it would be in here!"*

Technical people tend to like things that fit into a box. One plus one is two. Two multiplied by two is four. Red mixed with blue is purple. It is important to remember there are times things do not always fit into neat little boxes. For example, when tuning an Oracle database, it is important to keep in mind that database performance is more than the sum of the performance of its parts; e.g., server, I/O subsystem, application queries. There are complex interrelationships between these parts. The effective database tuner needs to be aware that 'cooperative changes' may be necessary.

Why should a DBA worry about things outside of the database? Is it not enough to demonstrate that the database is fine, and let the system administrators worry about things like operating system tuning, and network engineers worry about network capacity issues?

First, in some places, the same person does some or all of these jobs. Regardless, when management hears about a performance problem, they do not care who fixes the problem; just that it gets fixed.

Secondly, it is much more satisfying to be a part of a solution than to simply say "it's not a problem with the database." Being a part of the solution is also a better career option, because management generally prefers team players that participate in finding solutions rather than simply passing the 'hot potato' to the next department.

Definition

There has been as much written about different tuning approaches as has been written about different dieting techniques. There are books about the protein diet, the melon diet, the cabbage diet and even the ice-cream diet just to name a few. Likewise, there are many books and sources for different ideas on tuning databases. Some of them are based on facts. Others are based on testing that may have worked or appeared to work under specific circumstances, but as far as a day-in and day-out methodology, they work about as well as the ice-cream diet does for someone trying to lose weight. It is possible too that some of these misguided approaches may have been based on older versions of Oracle and are no longer effective methods of enhancing performance.

Trying to implement a tuning project that includes wildly different schools of thought is a recipe for chaos. "Increase the buffer cache to increase the buffer cache hit ratio." "Increase the *sort_area_size* parameter so more sorts can be done in memory." "Add more CPUs since the idle time for the host has vanished." "Migrate to a new machine since more RAM is needed to support the larger SGA needed to accommodate the larger buffer size."

In the end, the problem has still not been fixed and frustrated users are still calling because the "database is still too slow." And now, the system administrators are saying that it cannot be a system problem since they just installed a million dollars worth of equipment. To make matters worse, since the recommendations have not done any good; convincing people that any future changes have any chance of working is now much more difficult. All of the changes might have been good in isolation, but by neglecting the whole system, each change either improved nothing or made something else suffer.

The solution to this problem is simple. Make and recommend only changes that will fix the problem and make the database run more efficiently. If only it were that simple. But applying some of the concepts introduced in this book can make it much easier. These concepts will help identify what the bottleneck is in the system, which will then lead to determining what needs to be changed to improve performance. These concepts will be presented and expanded upon through the rest of this book and there will be examples provided showing their ease of use.

One way to think of tuning in a holistic manner is to remember everything that could be changed, whether it is database parameters, server specifications, or application/code enhancements to name a few, might only be addressing a symptom and not the underlying cause of the performance problem.

For instance, consider the scenario where the CPUs have very little idle time. The decision is made that a CPU upgrade is needed. Unfortunately, the CPUs were not the underlying cause of the slowness the users were experiencing. Now, when the additional (or faster) CPUs are brought online, I/O requests or buffer gets, or whatever the actual cause for the slowness are now processed faster and the users start screaming even louder since the system upgrade has actually made the system slower.

By using wait analysis to look for the cause of the slowness, instead of just identifying symptoms, the problem can be fixed instead of merely treating the symptoms. The Wait Interface provides a look at the whole system from a database perspective in order to and find the root cause instead of seeing only database symptoms.

Proactive STATSPACK Tuning

It is possible to use STATSPACK to keep track of statistics and with some well chosen scripts find out as soon as important measurements get out-of-line. STATSPACK is a package that comes with Oracle databases that can capture current data from the dynamic performance views identified by *v$*. It is possible then to report on this data for any period of time where a collection was captured. The benefit is that a time slot from day-to-day or week-to-week can be analyzed and action can be taken if any issues surface.

Script alerts from STATSPACK can potentially allow the DBA an opportunity to start diagnosis of a problem even before the users notice there is one. Even better, being able to diagnose and fix the problem before the users even notice the problem. Being the un-sung hero is a much better option that being noticed in a negative way. This may mean a little extra effort on the part of the DBA to make certain management sees and understands these un-noticed efforts.

Installing *STATSPACK* is as easy as running a script while connected as *sysdba* and following the prompts. With UNIX, the script is named *spcreate.sql* and it is located in *$ORACLE_HOME/rdbms/admin*. Once it is installed, schedule a regular snapshot using *statspack.snap* that fits the system environment. Consider running it hourly, around the clock, or every 15 minutes during peak business processes, just so long as whatever interval is chosen fits system needs. It will be necessary to monitor for space usage. If the scheduled collections occur every 15 minutes around the clock, plan on allocating a lot of space to the tablespace where the PERFSTAT user was placed. Also, clean up snapshots that are no longer needed. Housekeeping such as this is imperative to avoid the risk of running out of space and consequently being noticed by users or management in a most unfavorable light.

STATSPACK has reports already built-in to access the data gathered by the utility. Custom programs can also be written. These custom scripts can look for certain conditions that have been issues in the system environment, like I/O bottlenecks for instance. Or they can report trends while leaving it up to the DBA to determine if there is a problem.

If baseline measurements have been established, detecting changes in normal system operations should be straightforward. Having custom scripts in place permit notification before the users ever notice a drop in performance.

Reactive STATSPACK Tuning

Being proactive is always a better idea than being reactive, but there are times when there is not a choice. It is a good idea to work towards a rigorous code review for all application changes. However, predicting when an ad-hoc query user is going to run a query that will do a full-table scan on every table in the database before it joins 10 of them may not be possible. It also may not be possible to determine when a system component starts to fail causing a network flood.

It is in cases like these when STATSPACK shows that it is a great tool for reactive tuning in a holistic environment. Provided the right elements are reviewed, it does a good job of pointing out where in the whole system the problems are being experienced.

For example, the "File IO Stats" section of the STATSPACK report will indicate if the file system is causing a delay in writing to disk. Using this section, it will be possible to see if the delay is limited to a certain mount point or tablespace. With this information, choose whether to dig deeper into either the OS with tools like *iostat*, or the database level, to determine where the problem is and what action is needed to resolve it. Case studies in the following chapters will demonstrate.

If baseline measurements have been established, it will be possible to detect changes from normal system operations. This will help determine what changed and is causing the system to run slower. It could be a change in executes per parse rates, an increase in the number of library cache invalidations, or a jump in the wait time for a specific tablespace. These changes could be triggered by a code change in the application, a new user running wild queries against the database, or even another DBA taking a backup to the same disk or mount point as a vital tablespace uses.

In reactive tuning does not allow for the luxury of time. In order to restore business to normal operations, it is necessary to identify the cause of the slowness in order to implement possible resolutions quickly. This makes a resource like www.oraperf.com vital. There is no fee to access this site; just register for a free account. This site provides access to a program designed by Anjo Kolk, one of the leaders in using the Wait Interface. Upload a *STATSPACK* report to this site, and within a very short time an interactive analysis is returned that helps identify where the majority of time is spent; whether it's waiting for a resource or working. This analysis allows exploration into the major causes for delay quickly and efficiently with just a few mouse clicks. This resource does not replace the need for an established baseline. But, it would likely help if one does not exist and an urgent fix is needed.

Ratio-Based Tuning

Ever heard "a low buffer cache hit ratio 'makes' the system slow?" That 'fact' has been proven wrong many times and in different ways. A favorite procedure was posted by a DBA on the Oracle-l mailing list and states that BCHR can be increased to nearly any number desired by simply retrieving large amounts of data repeatedly. This will inflate the BCHR by increasing the number of consistent gets. A copy of this procedure is available on Connor McDonald's web site; http://www.oracledba.co.uk.

For a more comprehensive discussion on why a high BCHR is not good, please see Cary Millsap's paper, "*Why 99% Cache Hit Ratio Is Not OK*" at http://www.hotsos.com. Metalink Note 33883.1 provides an explanation as well as one of the possible explanations for the high hit ratio. "A hit ratio close to 100% does not mean the application is good. It is quite possible to get an excellent hit ratio by using a very unselective index in a heavily used SQL statement." This would be an undesirable way to achieve a high BCHR.

By focusing on how to use ratios when looking at the whole system instead of just at the database, there are some instances where a ratio makes some sense. When required sorts occur in a database and memory is able to handle them, there is generally no problem. On the other hand, when a required sort happens that is too big for the *sort_area_size*, Oracle uses the temporary tablespace as temporary storage and registers it as a sort to disk. It is nice that the RDBMS is able to complete the sort, but the cost in time for a query that requires a sort to disk is significantly higher than one that is done in memory. Consequently, performance is suboptimal.

Since tuning involves finding processes that are suboptimal and making them better so they are at least closer to optimal, knowing when there are sorts to disk would be beneficial. *sorts_ratio.sql* is one quick check to do when the system is suddenly slow.

🖫 sorts_ratio.sql

```
-- *******************************************************
-- Copyright © 2003 by Rampant TechPress
-- This script is free for non-commercial purposes
-- with no warranties.  Use at your own risk.
--
-- To license this script for a commercial purpose,
-- contact info@rampant.cc
-- *******************************************************

/* sorts_ratio.sql */
select
   NAME,
   VALUE
from
   V$SYSSTAT
where
   NAME in (
   'sorts (memory)',
   'sorts (disk)'
   );
```

```
NAME              VALUE
---------------   -------------
sorts (memory)    5,626,201
sorts (disk)      4,059
```

From this data it can be seen that the ratio in this case is less than 1% (4059 / 5626201). Unless our sort to disk count is off the charts right now compared to the previous portion of the database uptime, there is probably not a sort to disk problem. If

---

there was a problem, more research would be warranted to see if there is a session or area in the application that is causing a large percentage of sorts to disk.

If the problem is a query that can be tuned to avoid a sort without affecting the results, that would be better than increasing the *sort_area_size*. Increasing the default *sort_area_size* for the database would impact all users and would increase the demand on the physical memory that could, depending on the number of concurrent users, exhaust the physical memory of the machine. If that happens, the performance will drop further, because the system may have started paging and swapping.

The *v$sysstat* performance view is only a counter. If the database has been up for any significant length of time, these numbers will not be helpful unless this view is queried periodically and it is known that earlier in the day there were only 20 sorts to disk. Of course, using *stats$* tables with snapshot data makes this query a bit more complicated. However, it would permit narrowing down the data so the disk to memory ratio for sorts could be seen from the previous hour, 10 minutes, or whatever increment is being used to collect STATSPACK data. This would enable permit aggressive exploration into where all the disk sorts are coming from, or permit searching for another culprit that is impacting the system.

It may be a more complicated script, but if STATSPACK is being run on a regular basis, a script like *sp_sorts_ratio.sql* can confirm or deny whether there are sort-related performance issues.

🖫 sp_sorts_ratio.sql

```
--  ****************************************************
-- Copyright © 2003 by Rampant TechPress
-- This script is free for non-commercial purposes
-- with no warranties.  Use at your own risk.
--
```

```
-- To license this script for a commercial purpose,
-- contact info@rampant.cc
-- ************************************************

/* sp_sorts_ratio.sql */
column SNAP_DATE heading "Year Mo Day Hour" format a16
column MEMORY_SORTS                         format 999,999,999
column DISK_SORTS                           format 999,999,999
column "DISK/MEMORY RATIO"                  format 999.99
select
   to_char(SNAP_TIME, 'yyyy-mm-dd HH24') SNAP_DATE,
   MEMNEW.VALUE-MEMOLD.VALUE MEMORY_SORTS,
   DISKNEW.VALUE-DISKOLD.VALUE DISK_SORTS,
   (((DISKNEW.VALUE-DISKOLD.VALUE) /
   (MEMNEW.VALUE-MEMOLD.VALUE)) * 100)
   "DISK/MEMORY RATIO"
from
   PERFSTAT.STATS$SYSSTAT MEMOLD,
   PERFSTAT.STATS$SYSSTAT MEMNEW,
   PERFSTAT.STATS$SYSSTAT DISKNEW,
   PERFSTAT.STATS$SYSSTAT DISKOLD,
   PERFSTAT.STATS$SNAPSHOT sp
where
   DISKNEW.SNAP_ID = sp.SNAP_ID
and
   DISKOLD.SNAP_ID = sp.SNAP_ID-1
and
   MEMNEW.SNAP_ID = sp.SNAP_ID
and
   MEMOLD.SNAP_ID = sp.SNAP_ID-1
and
   MEMOLD.NAME = 'sorts (memory)'
and
   MEMNEW.NAME = 'sorts (memory)'
and
   DISKOLD.NAME = 'sorts (disk)'
and
   DISKNEW.NAME = 'sorts (disk)'
and
   MEMNEW.VALUE - MEMOLD.VALUE > 0
and
   DISKNEW.VALUE - DISKOLD.VALUE > 0
and
   trunc(sp.SNAP_TIME) > '&Start_Time_dd_mon_yy'
order by
   SNAP_DATE
;
```

```
SQL> @sp_sorts_ratio
Enter value for start_time_dd_mon_yy: 11-nov-03
old   35:    trunc(sp.SNAP_TIME) > '&Start_Time_dd_mon_yy'
new   35:    trunc(sp.SNAP_TIME) > '11-nov-03'

Year Mo Day Hour MEMORY_SORTS   DISK_SORTS DISK/MEMORY RATIO
---------------- ------------ ------------ -----------------
2003-11-20 21             593            1               .17
2003-11-29 18           1,008            1               .10
2003-11-29 18           1,538            1               .07
2003-11-29 19           1,445            1               .07
2003-11-29 19             999            3               .30
2003-11-29 20             780            2               .26
2003-11-29 21             915            1               .11
2003-11-29 22           1,066            3               .28

8 rows selected.
```

If the users were reporting sluggish system performance around 7 pm on the 29th, there were 2 or 3 of the sorts that went to disk. The ratio did increase by around 300%, but a ratio of .3% is still nothing to start worrying about. Given these factors, it is not likely that the user response time issues are related to sorts going to disk.

This query is one example of how to extend the use of STATSPACK beyond the built-in *spreport.sql*. Chapter 7 will go into more detail on how to use STATSPACK wait information. For more information and help on maximizing the use of STATSPACK in general, read "Oracle 9i, High-Performance Tuning with STATSPACK" by Donald Burleson.

One other area where ratios may make sense is the buffer pool. However, this would only apply where multiple pools have been implemented, and then only if the keep pool is high. It is OK for the recycle pool to be low. These values should be measured against baseline statistics and not against a fixed value. If the values change dramatically one way or the other, look into the Wait Events to try and determine the cause. See the output from *buffer_pool_ratio.sql* below for a sample of this measurement.

```
-- ****************************************************
-- Copyright © 2003 by Rampant TechPress
-- This script is free for non-commercial purposes
-- with no warranties.  Use at your own risk.
--
-- To license this script for a commercial purpose,
-- contact info@rampant.cc
-- ****************************************************

/* buffer_pool_ratio.sql */
column RATIO format 999.99
column NAME  format a15

select
   NAME,
   100 *
   (1 -
   (PHYSICAL_READS/
   (DB_BLOCK_GETS + CONSISTENT_GETS)
   )) "RATIO"
from
   V$BUFFER_POOL_STATISTICS;
```

```
SQL> @buffer_pool_ratio

NAME             RATIO
---------------  -------
KEEP              61.86
RECYCLE           99.03
DEFAULT           97.19
```

Ways of properly configuring the buffer pool will be discussed in a later chapter. An explanation will also be given for why the output listed above is sub-optimal.

Tuning Disk I/O

One problem area that may surface during a tuning project is I/O. The time it takes the database to read and/or write to a file may be causing performance issues. In order to have the information necessary for a productive meeting with the System Administrator, gather *v$filestat* statistics on the time it takes to read and write to the file system. The script *io_report.sql* looks at the data stored in *v$filestat* and calculates the average amount of time the operating system has taken to satisfy each request. This script shows how to use the average number to determine if the response time is too high for a given mount point. It is possible that the mount point is getting saturated with activity due to an inefficient query. An average number that is too high for a specific mount point could be an indicator of a file system that has saturated its I/O throughput capacity. This could also be an area for the system administrators to fix. For example, if a controller has gone bad causing all I/O requests to go through the backup card, the result would be twice the traffic.

🖫 io_report.sql

```
--   ****************************************************
-- Copyright © 2003 by Rampant TechPress
-- This script is free for non-commercial purposes
-- with no warranties.  Use at your own risk.
--
-- To license this script for a commercial purpose,
-- contact info@rampant.cc
--   ****************************************************

/* io_report.sql */
column FILE_NAME   format a30
column PHYRDS      format 999,999
column PHYWRTS     format 999,999
column READTIM     format 999,999

select
   FILE_NAME,
   PHYRDS,
   READTIM,
   PHYWRTS,
   READTIM / (PHYRDS + 1) "READ AVG (ms)",
   PHYRDS + PHYWRTS "TOTAL I/O"
from
   V$FILESTAT a,
   DBA_DATA_FILES b
where
   a.FILE# = b.FILE_ID
and
   READTIM/(PHYRDS + 1) > 0.5
order by
   5,
   6;
```

```
FILE_NAME                        PHYRDS  READTIM  PHYWRTS READ AVG (ms)  TOTAL I/O
-----------------------------   -------- -------- -------- ------------- ----------
/oradata/TOY/system01.dbf         21,805   14,094    3,246  .646335871        25051
/oradata/TOY/users02.dbf          13,669    8,949   17,762  .654645208        31431
/oradata/TOY/rbs01.dbf             8,516    5,592   62,585  .656569215        71101
/oradata/TOY/users01.dbf          29,940   20,750   39,680  .693029625        69620
/oradata/TOY/index01.dbf             216      246      175 1.13364055           391
/oradata/TOY/rcvcat01.dbf            177      341      175 1.91573034           352

6 rows selected.
```

This script is a great way to monitor the performance of the I/O subsystem as seen by the database. It uses one of the *v$* views discussed earlier. *v$filestat* as well as *dba_data_files* are used to show the file name as well as the file id, which makes it easier to approach the storage administrators if necessary.

This particular version of the script focuses on the time it takes the I/O subsystem to perform a read when requested by the database, as well as the total I/O for any given data file. As such, it is useful if user complaints are query or lookup related, because it is a common cause.

If the bottleneck sounds like it is related to saving since users are making statements such as, "it takes a long time when I click the save button before I can go to the next record," then change PHYRDS to PHYWRTS in the read average calculation to see the write average. Also, the query can be written to always look at both ratios if this would provide a better analysis for the current environment. The system administrator should be able to explain what level of service users should expect to receive when accessing their systems. If not, encourage them to call the support number for their systems and find out. Short of that, simply provide the administrator with the analysis and explain that better response times are expected from the system.

For current SAN technology, 10ms or less should be a reasonable goal. Adjust the filter condition in the *io_report.sql* script according to a reasonable number for the current system.

Schedule this to run daily and e-mail/page the results when any data files approach or exceed that threshold.

Another way to utilize I/O statistics is using tools provided by the operating system. In Windows, *perfmon* provides a GUI to look at the loads on various components of the system. In UNIX, the most commonly available tools are *iostat* and *vmstat*; at least one of which is commonly available in command-line form in most UNIX distributions. *iostat* includes a device utilization report that provides statistics on a per physical device or partition basis. The statistics provided are for the whole system or device being examined, which may include database activity as well as any other activity on that device. This is another good reason for keeping database files separate from other files on the system.

It also strengthens the argument against mixing data files from multiple databases, since it may not be easy to determine which database or process is causing the load. *iostat* may signal that there is a large load, but good design will help quickly narrow down the cause. It will be necessary to review the *man* page on the appropriate platform for specific uses and implementation details.

Using Red Hat 7.3 in the example provided here, the first line of data represents the totals since system startup. Subsequent lines represent the statistics since the last line. For example, Figure 4.1 shows the results of running the *iostat –d 2 3* command. This means "run iostat on all devices every 2 seconds. Repeat 3 times." It displays three lines of data as well as the report and line header information. The statistics in the first line are for the total time the system has been up. The second and third line statistics represent the current system activity measured in 2-second intervals.

```
[oracle@matthew oracle]$ iostat -d 2 3
Linux 2.4.18-3 (matthew)       11/23/2003

Device:            tps    Blk_read/s    Blk_wrtn/s    Blk_read    Blk_wrtn
dev3-0            5.58        16.79          94.69    11583322    65336618

Device:            tps    Blk_read/s    Blk_wrtn/s    Blk_read    Blk_wrtn
dev3-0           43.50         0.00        1933.00           0        3866

Device:            tps    Blk_read/s    Blk_wrtn/s    Blk_read    Blk_wrtn
dev3-0            4.50         0.00          84.00           0         168
```

Figure 4.1 – *Sample of iostat*

vmstat is another common utility on UNIX systems. Use the *man* pages or other documentation and learn how to use this utility effectively.

If using a Microsoft operating system, take some time to determine what tools are available internally, or what third-party options are available. Research and test whatever tools available to make tuning more productive.

One of the technical reviewers for this book, Kevin Hedger, worked with to develop a Perl script that would make raw analysis of *iostat* dump files easier. This script, *io_stat_analysis.pl,* will need to be modified for many environments due to the variances in the way *iostat* output differs from version to version. Obviously, this will not work for Windows since *iostat* is a UNIX utility. It is possible to have *iostat* run with the data being copied to a text file. The objective is that this text file could then be analyzed to quickly determine whether the operating system was experiencing a high level of I/O activity.

This script breaks down the report by device and discards the initial data. The first device records consist of historical summaries and would skew the results. The script is named *io_stat_analysis.pl* and is also available in the code depot.

🖫 io_stat_analysis.pl

```perl
-- ***************************************************
-- Copyright © 2003 by Rampant TechPress
-- This script is free for non-commercial purposes
-- with no warranties.  Use at your own risk.
--
-- To license this script for a commercial purpose,
-- contact info@rampant.cc
-- ***************************************************

#!/usr/bin/perl -w

#This script will return an average per device.
# Author: Kevin Hedger
# Included here with permission

# Get arguments in
 $inputfile  = $ARGV[0];

#Run test for input
testInput();

sub testInput
{
   # my($inputfile);

    # If no arguments are entered show Usage and exit
    if(! $inputfile)
    {
       Usage();
       exit;
    }
}

sub Usage
{
   print "\nUsage:\n";
   print "Please enter the command in the following order\n";
   print "io_stat_analisys.pl [input file]\n";
   print "input file = /path/inputfile\n";
}



open (STATDATA, "$inputfile") || die("can't open file
$inputfile\n");

#Outout Header Format
printf "%-9s %12s %12s %12s %10s %10s\n", "", Average, Average,
Average, Average, Average;
printf "%-9s %12s %12s %12s %10s %10s\n", Device, Tps, Blk_read_s,
Blk_wrtn_s, Blk_read, Blk_wrtn;

#Read in input file and loop through.
```

Oracle Wait Event Tuning

```perl
while(<STATDATA>)
{ chomp;
   if(/^dev/)
   {
   ($device, $tps, $blkrs, $blkws, $blkr, $blkw) = split(/\s+/, $_);
   # Skips first device listings.
   if (! (defined $save{$device}))
      {
      $save{$device} = {};
      next;
      }
   #Populates Hash %save
   push @{$save{$device}{col1}}, $tps;
   push @{$save{$device}{col2}}, $blkrs;
   push @{$save{$device}{col3}}, $blkws;
   push @{$save{$device}{col4}}, $blkr;
   push @{$save{$device}{col5}}, $blkw;
   }
}
close(STATDATA);


foreach $device (sort keys %save)
{
#Returns the # of elements in the hash
$num_values_col1 = scalar(@{$save{$device}{col1}});
$num_values_col2 = scalar(@{$save{$device}{col2}});
$num_values_col3 = scalar(@{$save{$device}{col3}});
$num_values_col4 = scalar(@{$save{$device}{col4}});
$num_values_col5 = scalar(@{$save{$device}{col5}});

$total_col1 = 0;
$total_col2 = 0;
$total_col3 = 0;
$total_col4 = 0;
$total_col5 = 0;

   #Sums the values of the hash
   foreach (@{$save{$device}{col1}})
   {
   $total_col1 += $_;
   }

   foreach (@{$save{$device}{col2}})
   {
   $total_col2 += $_;
   }

   foreach (@{$save{$device}{col3}})
   {
   $total_col3 += $_;
   }

   foreach (@{$save{$device}{col4}})
   {
   $total_col4 += $_;
   }
```

```
foreach (@{$save{$device}{col5}})
{
$total_col5 += $_;
}

#Devides the value of the hash by the number of elements for and
average.
  $ave_col1 = $total_col1 / $num_values_col1;
  $ave_col2 = $total_col2 / $num_values_col2;
  $ave_col3 = $total_col3 / $num_values_col3;
  $ave_col4 = $total_col4 / $num_values_col4;
  $ave_col5 = $total_col5 / $num_values_col5;

#Formats the output data.
  printf "%-9s %12.2f %12.2f %12.2f %10.0f %10.0f\n", $device,
$ave_col1, $ave_col2, $ave_col3, $ave_col4, $ave_col5;
}
```

Figure 4.2 shows the first several lines from an *iostat*-generated text file. Note how dev11 only has values in the first line. This is because this device is not heavily used and was not used during the interval of this measurement.

```
Device:          tps     Blk_read/s   Blk_wrtn/s   Blk_read    Blk_wrtn
dev3-0          9.61         34.53       158.17     34841262   159606892
dev11-0         0.00          0.00         0.00          368           0

Device:          tps     Blk_read/s   Blk_wrtn/s   Blk_read    Blk_wrtn
dev3-0        190.00       8656.00     11628.00         8656       11628
dev11-0         0.00          0.00         0.00            0           0

Device:          tps     Blk_read/s   Blk_wrtn/s   Blk_read    Blk_wrtn
dev3-0         77.00        480.00       424.00          480         424
dev11-0         0.00          0.00         0.00            0           0

Device:          tps     Blk_read/s   Blk_wrtn/s   Blk_read    Blk_wrtn
dev3-0         50.00       3080.00      1824.00         3080        1824
dev11-0         0.00          0.00         0.00            0           0
```

Figure 4.2 – *Raw iostat data*

Figure 4.3 shows how dev11 has averages of 0 because the initial values are discarded since they do not apply to the current review period.

Oracle Wait Event Tuning

```
[oracle@matthew perl]$ ./io_stat_analisys.pl io_stat_raw
                Average      Average      Average     Average     Average
Device              Tps    Blk_read_s   Blk_wrtn_s   Blk_read   Blk_wrtn
dev11-0            0.00         0.00         0.00          0          0
dev3-0           117.01      4610.31      3371.53       4621       3375
```

Figure 4.3 – *Processed iostat data*

The processed results can be reviewed and compared to previous days. This will help determine whether the current performance issue is related to I/O performance. If so, this might mean I/O is causing the problem and the proper course of action is to determine if any storage configurations have been changed. More likely, there was a change to the application or how the users are using it and suddenly there are full table-scans where there used to be index reads. This could be overtaxing some component of the storage system.

Tuning SQL

When looking at a whole-system tuning approach, SQL analysis and tuning may be necessary. Whether SQL tuning in analyzing a performance issue is a factor will depend on the applications the organization is using and the experience and skill of the developers. Even with talented developers, their goal is to provide a working application. Therefore, tuning can take a back seat until the production users get to assess the scalability of the application and the DBA gets involved because "the database is slow."

"I wonder if I/O would be improved if we plugged these back in."

SQL tuning becomes a requirement when, after determining that the biggest bottleneck in the system is I/O and that the response time is lacking and impacting the users, it becomes apparent that enhancing the storage hardware is not the only solution. If the only change in system statistics is that the number of I/O operations has increased dramatically, and there is no corresponding business driver; i.e., acquisition, merger or sales spike, to account for this, there may be a new piece of code or old statistics that are causing unnecessary I/O operations.

The Oracle Optimizer is used to determine the best way to access the data. It works in two modes, Rule and Cost. Rule-based Optimization (RBO) has a set of rules it follows to determine the best execution plan. The Cost Based Optimizer (CBO) determines the best way to access the data based on the relative cost of different execution plans.

Before version 8i, the CBO was not always as smart as an average DBA, so hints were often needed. Hints provided the DBA a way to influence the optimizer toward more efficient execution plans. Gradually, the CBO has gotten more efficient to the point where now a hint rarely results in a better execution plan.

If it is determined that there is some 'bad' SQL that needs to be tuned, there are several possible target areas:

- Reduce or eliminate unnecessary I/O, which is commonly done by eliminating a full table-scan. Sometimes the most efficient execution plan is to use a full table-scan, so elimination of full table-scans may not be recommended.

- Appropriate index creation and usage is important. If there is an index that can never be used effectively, then it should be dropped. If there are several indexes, it might make sense to combine them into a single concatenated index.

- Use the buffer cache when I/O is appropriate and required. If there are several small tables that are frequently accessed, and they do not all fit in the buffer cache, increase it if they are the source of a performance problem.

- Reduce excessive parsing. This is not necessarily a SQL tuning issue, but if a PL/SQL loop is designed poorly, parsing could result every time through a loop when it is not needed.

There are other factors involved in tuning SQL. Since there are already good books on the subject, this book will not go into a great deal of detail in this area. This book will focus on identifying 'bad' SQL with the Wait Interface when that is the cause of a performance problem in the database.

Network Tuning

Recall how frustrating it can be to be stuck in traffic with a perfectly good vehicle that can only use a fraction of its potential.

It does not matter if it has a V-8 engine with over 200 horsepower; the capacity bottleneck of the expressway still exists. In the Oracle world SQL*Net waits are the wait events that express the traffic jam on the network. Due to the nature of TCP/IP communication, there will always be some waits, just as when there is no traffic, it still takes some amount of time to travel from one place to another. SQL*Net waits are experienced by the vehicles in Figure 4.4 as they have to wait for everyone ahead in order to get to their destination. Everyone has to wait. The key is making sure that the waits are not causing delays in the rest of the database.

Figure 4.4 – *SQL*Net Waits*

When a user queries a database, from the time the query is sent till the time the first part of the data is returned, the session is waiting. This is session wait time which includes the time the data is being gathered from the database and all the while it is being sent across the network. This wait event can be examined to see if it is out of line for the current system configuration, or if it has grown by leaps and bounds in the past day as an indication of network problems or a surge in business.

For example, the week after the Thanksgiving holiday, many stores have a sale to kick off the Holiday shopping season. On that day, an online retailer who is having a sale may very well see a large spike in SQL*Net waits, but that will correspond to the surge in customer sessions and hopefully, sales. System Administrators will also be monitoring their network to make sure it is capable of handling the expected surge in traffic. Therefore, the increase in SQL*Net waits will not necessarily be indicative of a deterioration of user response time. It could just be an indicator that there are more customers seeing the "normal" network response time.

This is one of the reasons why 10046 tracing has an important role to play. If the total database SQL*Net waits has increased in proportion to the increase in user volume, then there may not be a problem. However, if the increase of SQL*Net waits is disproportionately impacting one activity such as merchandise check-out, then a 10046 trace on that activity should indicate the source of problem.

When a user queries the database with an update command, there will be an interval of time in between the time the user gets a prompt back, and when they commit the transaction. This is the wait time where the database is waiting for the user. This type of wait cannot really be tuned short of designing the application to automatically commit changes or rollback if the user does not take action within a specified time frame. But, not being able to tune this is really not a problem since the only user impacted, outside of any locking issues, is the one causing the problem. That is why many sources refer to SQL*Net waits as "idle waits" and recommend ignoring them.

There are some tools that a DBA should keep handy in order to help assess whether or not the performance problem is network-related. *netstat* is one of these tools. *netstat* displays network-related data in various formats depending on what parameters or options are used when it is invoked. For example, *netstat –a | grep 1521* will produce a list of all connections to this host involving the default listener port of 1521. This can be seen in Figure 4.5. If there is a network-related issue, the information gathered here will help the network administrators when tracking down the source of the problem.

```
[oracle@matthew oracle]$ netstat -a | grep 1521
tcp        0        0 *:1521                    *:*                     LISTEN
tcp        0        0 matthew:1521              192.168.2.101:1463      ESTABLISHED
tcp        0        0 matthew:1130              matthew:1521            ESTABLISHED
tcp        0        0 matthew:1521              192.168.2.101:1375      ESTABLISHED
tcp        0        0 matthew:1521              matthew:1130            ESTABLISHED
```

Figure 4.5 – *Network information for port 1521*

There are a few ways to tune the network to reduce the impact that SQL*Net waits will have. One way is to tune the physical layer. This could mean increasing the number of network cards or changing them to a faster technology. This could also be done with a faster Wide Area Network (WAN) connection. In a Local Area Network (LAN) environment, this may mean changing from CAT5 to CAT6 or to Fiber.

Another way to tune the network is to tune the logical layer. This would involve changing the configuration network to use different packet sizes. Net8 communication allows configuration of the Session Data Unit and Transport Data Unit. This is done with the SDU and TDU parameters in the Net8 configuration files. This tuning needs to be done in conjunction with the network settings, so set these values to the most effective sizes otherwise less effective network utilization could result. One way of gathering this information is by using the *netstat* command with the *–i* flag. This is shown in Figure 4.6. The ee# or eth# entries will indicate what the MTU (Maximum Transmission Unit) is, which is one of the pieces of information needed in order to calculate the settings for the SDU and TDU parameters.

```
[oracle@matthew oracle]$ netstat -i
Kernel Interface table
Iface   MTU Met   RX-OK RX-ERR RX-DRP RX-OVR    TX-OK TX-ERR TX-DRP TX-OVR Flg
eth0   1500   0   89621      0      0      0    45021      0      0      0 BMRU
lo    16436   0    1962      0      0      0     1962      0      0      0 LRU
```

Figure 4.6 – *Using Netstat to determine SDU/TDU*

SQL*Net tuning can be a challenging topic, so it will not be covered extensively here. Oracle has many valuable references including Document ID 1018693.6 How can SQL*Net performance be improved, and 1005123.6 Tuning SQL*Net for better performance. These should help if it is determined that there is a network-related problem that needs to be tuned from Oracle.

Another way to get this information is to communicate with the network group or system administration group. Obtaining information this way helps keep communications open with these groups, which is a good idea.

Regardless of the way the information is obtained, make sure that these values are set correctly since having the network use larger packet sizes will help performance. Since every network packet has overhead; larger packets will result in fewer packets, and therefore less network-related overhead. Unless the packets are sized too large and they end up getting split up which will create more network-related overhead, so be careful.

The last way to tune the network is reducing the number and size of the database accesses. This boils down to tuning SQL. By making efficient use of the database through reducing unnecessary data requests; there will be less traffic, and the remaining network traffic will get through with less delays.

There are important things to consider when tuning the network. One of which is to only work on it if the results from the wait analysis indicate that there is a problem. Another very important item is that if tuning in this arena is required, undertaking this alone as the DBA is not recommended. Work with someone in the networking group to get an understanding of the existing network configuration and what options are available for changing it.

System Tuning

This chapter is covering holistic or system-wide tuning. In this section, when system tuning is referenced, the focus is server specific tuning. The two biggest items in this area are memory and processor.

When systems are slow, one of the possible causes is simple lack of horsepower. CPUs that have little or no idle time might indicate the need for new hardware, either more CPUs or faster ones, or maybe even both. A CPU with little or no idle time could be the symptom of a hard working machine being asked to do too much. If this were the case, then a CPU upgrade would be a good idea and would likely speed things up for the end user. Other times, the CPU is spending its time on busy work that is not necessary. Things like excess parsing use up CPU cycles when they are not adding any value.

A key to tuning systems is making effective use of their key resources; primarily CPU and RAM. The first step towards effective utilization of these resources is the understanding how much and in what manner they are being used. In UNIX environments, one of the tools available is *top*. *top* is a display of the processes that are using CPU resources. Figure 4.7 is a sample of what *top* looks like.

```
 oracle@matthew:~
 9:55pm  up 4 days, 23:00,  4 users,  load average: 9.69, 3.57, 1.55
126 processes: 115 sleeping, 11 running, 0 zombie, 0 stopped
CPU states: 91.3% user,  6.9% system,  0.0% nice,  1.7% idle
Mem:   126804K av,  122028K used,    4776K free,       0K shrd,     2860K buff
Swap: 1020088K av,  139700K used,  880388K free                   56204K cached

  PID USER     PRI  NI   SIZE   RSS  SHARE STAT %CPU %MEM   TIME COMMAND
 7027 root      16   0   7772  4476   2364 R    19.0  3.5 104:19 rhn-applet
 8082 oracle    17   0  15784  15M  14632 R    13.7 12.4  0:03 oracle
 8099 oracle    17   0  13124  12M  11972 R    11.3 10.3  0:05 oracle
 8086 oracle    15   0  15808  15M  14656 S     9.8 12.4  0:03 oracle
 8081 oracle    16   0  15504  15M  14352 R     6.0 12.2  0:03 oracle
 8089 oracle    15   0  13340  13M  12156 S     5.2 10.5  0:04 oracle
 8096 oracle    15   0  13068  12M  11916 S     4.9 10.3  0:03 oracle
 7806 oracle    16   0   1048  1048    792 R     4.3  0.8  0:14 top
 8083 oracle    15   0  13488  13M  12292 S     3.0 10.6  0:04 oracle
 8106 oracle    16   0  12940  12M  11788 S     3.0 10.2  0:04 oracle
 8090 oracle    17   0  12800  12M  11648 R     1.3 10.0  0:03 oracle
 1578 root      15   0  15308  2468   1596 S     0.9  1.9  0:34 X
 8095 oracle    18   0  14080  13M  12928 R     0.5 11.1  0:03 oracle
    5 root      15   0      0     0      0 SW    0.3  0.0  0:13 kswapd
 7855 oracle    17   0  17508  17M  16324 S     0.3 13.8  2:48 oracle
 1556 oracle    16   0   3604  2400   2276 R     0.1  1.8  1:37 oracle
 6977 root      15   0   3816  2852   2232 S     0.1  2.2  0:05 panel
```

Figure 4.7 *top running on a busy system*

By default, running *top* by itself on a command line will show summary statistics for the CPU and memory usage. In Figure 4.7, the system only has 1.7% idle CPU time, and it has 4,776 kb of free memory (RAM). In this case, the first thing to do is identify what is using 91.3% of the CPU. *top* displays the top processes, so first look into the processes with process ID's (PID's) of 7027, 8082 and 8099 as they are the top-3 CPU users.

In addition to *top*, *sar* is another commonly available tool to examine and monitor memory and CPU utilization. Both are available on many variants of UNIX and merit some attention for a better understanding of these valuable tools. In order to learn how to benefit from these tools, review their *man* pages or other documentation.

Business Tuning

Now before getting confused and starting to think that this is going to be a business process re-engineering book, relax. While the organization may require a process overhaul to become more efficient, the business tuning referred to here is only in the areas that are interacted with. It is here, when the 'softer skills' of business knowledge and political skills are needed.

Business knowledge is needed for many reasons. First of all, if the business and its processes are understood, it will be possible to quickly identify processes that do not add value to the organization and work to remove them, or at least reschedule them to accommodate more crucial work better.

When the cause of a system performance problem has been isolated and a solid understanding of the business exists, it will be easier to answer the question, "Is this query or report really necessary?" Another reason that knowledge of the business is beneficial is that when tuning SQL or making recommendations for application revisions, knowing how the users use the information will be invaluable when determining things like whether a bitmap index will help performance or hurt it.

Political skills are important when it comes to presenting findings to management. Knowing when to fight for a recommendation and when to accept a compromise solution will help keep management happy. It also has the potential benefit of providing credibility so next time an issue arises where a compromise will not provide the performance that the business requires, the recommendations will be taken seriously.

The last piece of business tuning to mention is that the key to a well performing database lies not in having the best tuning scripts, the best GUI tuning tool, the best database initialization parameters, the best operating system kernel settings or even the best tuning book. The key to an optimized database lies in having a database and application that were designed with the intended use in mind. All the tuning books, tips, seminars, scripts and tools are reactive when compared to an application that was built with a solid understanding of what the business needed the tool for, and how they wanted to use it.

Conclusion

The DBA cannot undertake this task of tuning the performance of a database by looking at the database in isolation. The title of this chapter is "The Importance of Holistic Tuning." It is imperative to work on balancing the requirements of the database with the available resources. Address the things that are hurting database performance rather than picking a target and "fixing" something that might not be broken; and probably will not help make the database performance complaints go away. This may often involve working with others, outside of the DBA group, as a team on the system as a whole.

The next chapters will go into detail on using Wait Analysis to determine where the database is hurting. The examples and case studies will provide material on how to apply the concepts discussed so far in a practical way by using the wait interface, 10046 trace and STATSPACK.

Using the Wait Interface

Defining the Wait Interface

Chapter 2 introduced the Wait Interface environment, so this chapter will touch briefly on defining it. Following that, will be how to productively use it. After showing the basic methodology, case studies will be presented that show samples of how to apply that methodology to track down and resolve various types of problems.

The Wait Interface is an internal part of the Oracle database that allows the DBA to see what component of the database is experiencing a bottleneck. The nature of bottlenecks is that there will always be at least one component of a system which prevents operations or processes from happening faster. If there is any hope of making the system faster, that bottleneck must be correctly identified. If there is not a problem with the current or forecast performance of the system, then identification of the bottleneck serves as a preventative measure. Someday down the road when the users complain about a performance problem, the baseline will be available to compare to the new bottleneck. This can often give insight into the cause of the current problem.

The Wait Interface is very effective when searching for performance bottlenecks.

The wait interface is made up of several dynamic performance views; primarily, *v$system_event, v$session_event* and *v$session_wait*. They can be used in various ways to dig into the system to search for the bottleneck that is impacting system performance.

Using the Wait Interface

So why would anyone want to look at these performance views anyway? Just like there are some people who like to take things apart to see what's inside, some people just want to know what makes the Oracle database "tick." However, most are more interested is keeping their bosses and the end users happy. If keeping everyone happy is the goal, this book is a great place to learn how to solve performance problems. For the clinically curious, this book is also a great place since knowing how to use these views to solve problems is a good starting point for doing further research.

There are several ways to use the Wait Interface to identify the cause for a system slowdown. One way is using a set of start/stop tables that are created and then dropped when data review is complete. This way helps reduce the inherent inaccuracies in the Wait Interface in the cumulative numbers gathered by some of the tables. Refer to the *start_system_events.sql*, *finish_system_events.sql* and *difference_system_events.sql* in Chapter 2. Examples can be found in the case study section of this chapter.

Another way to use the Wait Interface is to look directly at *v$session_wait*. This approach works well when there is a specific user or process that is running slower than usual or slower than is required to meet business requirements.

🖫 session_waits.sql

```
-- ***************************************************
-- Copyright © 2003 by Rampant TechPress
-- This script is free for non-commercial purposes
-- with no warranties.  Use at your own risk.
--
-- To license this script for a commercial purpose,
-- contact info@rampant.cc
-- ***************************************************

/* session_waits.sql */
column SID              format 999
column EVENT            format a28
column P1TEXT           format a15
column P3TEXT           format a8
column P2TEXT           format a8
column SECONDS_IN_WAIT  format 99999 heading SECONDS|IN_WAIT
column WAIT_TIME        format 999 heading WAIT|TIME
column STATE            format a18
column P1               format 999999999999
column P2               format 9999
column P3               format 99

select
   SID,
   EVENT,
   P1TEXT,
```

```
   P1,
   P2TEXT,
   P2,
   P3TEXT,
   P3,
   WAIT_TIME,
   SECONDS_IN_WAIT,
   STATE
from
   V$SESSION_WAIT
where
   EVENT not in (
      select
         EVENT
      from
         STATS$IDLE_EVENT)
order by
   WAIT_TIME,
   SECONDS_IN_WAIT;
```

Note that in versions as recent as 9.2.0.3, this query sometimes returns a high number of rows with "null event." Do not automatically reject or ignore these rows. It seems Oracle 9i has a bug that misclassifies some valid wait events as "null event." Bug # 1743159 was mentioned in Chapter 2, so check Metalink for an updated status of this and other bugs.

Step-By-Step Examples and Case Studies

Case #1. Failure to Use Bind Variables

In order to get a feeling for the overall system, such as whether it has latch free issues or excessive waits for file reads or writes, the following scripts will provide a good idea of where the problem lies. An event with a couple hundred occurrences is probably not the cause of a problem. On the other hand, any 'non-idle' wait that happened 30 million times, probably merits some attention. The next steps will help nail down the specific cause of the problem.

To tackle this problem, first run *show_system_events.sql* and *show_system_events2.sql*. The output is shown in Figures 5.1 and 5.2 respectively.

EVENT	TOT WAITS	TIME WAITED	AVG
io done	30,302,049	53,898,573	2.00
enqueue	70,986	2,747,451	39.00
async disk IO	5,913,927	1,646,095	.00
latch free	2,672,350	899,243	.00
rdbms ipc reply	44,279	33,624	1.00
inactive session	253	27,190	107.00
process startup	926	10,296	11.00
slave exit	337	3,001	9.00
wait list latch free	38	63	2.00
reliable message	1	0	.00

Figure 5.1 – *System-wide events by time waited*

EVENT	TOT WAITS	TIME WAITED	AVG
inactive session	253	27,190	107.00
enqueue	70,986	2,747,451	39.00
process startup	926	10,296	11.00
slave exit	337	3,001	9.00
wait list latch free	38	63	2.00
io done	30,302,049	53,898,573	2.00
rdbms ipc reply	44,279	33,624	1.00
latch free	2,672,429	899,252	.00
reliable message	1	0	.00
async disk IO	5,913,927	1,646,095	.00

Figure 5.2 – *System-wide events by average time*

Notice the similarity of the events in these two figures. This demonstrates that either of these scripts will point out the biggest wait events which have occurred on the system. The time waited sorted report (Figure 5.1, *show_system_events.sql*) helps to identify the scale or magnitude of difference between these events. The average time waited sorted report (Figure 5.2, *show_system_events2.sql*) helps identify the impact on each occurrence.

After getting a feel for the system by looking at the output from the previous scripts, it is time to start narrowing down the scope. Run *session_event_users.sql* to see which users are spending the most time waiting, and what events they are waiting for.

🖫 **session_event_users.sql**

```
--  ****************************************************
--  Copyright © 2003 by Rampant TechPress
--  This script is free for non-commercial purposes
--  with no warranties.  Use at your own risk.
--
--  To license this script for a commercial purpose,
--  contact info@rampant.cc
--  ****************************************************

/* session_event_users.sql */
column USERNAME            format a8
column EVENT               format a30
column SID                 format 9999
column AVERAGE_WAIT        format 99999 head "AVG|WAIT"
column TOTAL_WAITS         format 99999 head "TOTAL|WAITS"
column TOTAL_TIMEOUTS      format 9999 head "TOTAL|TIME|OUTS"
column TIME_WAITED         format 999999 head "TIME|WAITED"
column MAX_WAIT            format 99999 head "MAX|WAIT"
column TIME_WAITED_MICRO format 9999999 head "TIME|WAITED|MICRO"
set pagesize 100

select
   b.USERNAME,
   a.*
from
   V$SESSION_EVENT a,
   V$SESSION b
where
   a.SID = b.SID
and
   b.USERNAME is not null
order by
   AVERAGE_WAIT DESC;
```

USERNAME	SID	EVENT	TOTAL WAITS	TOTAL TIMEOUTS	TIME WAITED	AVG WAIT	MAX WAIT
MIGUELMA	211	library cache pin	12	11	3,569	297	322
GARRETMA	329	library cache pin	2	0	321	161	321
CRAIGCH	337	log file switch completion	2	0	5	3	4
ACEVEDAB	394	latch free	4	0	10	2	6
YAGACGE	369	enqueue	4	0	8	2	4

Figure 5.3 – *Users with top time waited*

Figure 5.3 shows that the single userid with the most time waited is MIGUELMA; with close to 100 hours. That may seem absurd, but knowing this user runs batch jobs and is logged in for days at a time clears up that misunderstanding.

Also, note the top two users have both spent time waiting for the same thing, library cache pin. Remember, latch free waits appeared in Figure 5.1 with over 2 million waits. One cause of "latch free" waits is the "library cache pin" so this confirms the information seen earlier.

Now that what is being waited on is known, the question becomes why? One reason this could be happening is the shared pool is improperly configured or sized. Another possible cause is failure to use bind variables.

There are also bugs that can cause this behavior. Among them is bug #2997330 which offers this suggestion: "Oracle support must be contacted if the problem persists, without a visible reason."

The next action to take in this case would be to examine the code this user is running. This can be easily done with the SID that is shown in the previous output and the *show_session_sql.sql* script.

🖫 show_session_sql.sql

```
--    ****************************************************
-- Copyright © 2003 by Rampant TechPress
-- This script is free for non-commercial purposes
-- with no warranties.  Use at your own risk.
--
-- To license this script for a commercial purpose,
-- contact info@rampant.cc
--    ****************************************************

/* show_session_sql.sql */
select
```

```
    SQL_TEXT
from
    V$SQLTEXT
where
    HASH_VALUE in (
        select
            SQL_HASH_VALUE
        from
            V$SESSION
        where
            SID = '&sid')
order by
    PIECE;
```

```
SQL> @show_session_sql
Enter value for sid: 211
old  12:          SID = '&sid')
new  12:          SID = '211')

SQL_TEXT
----------------------------------------------------------------
SELECT count(*) from   web_hits where   status = 55
```

Since it appears that this query is not using bind variables, the best solution may be to work with developers and change the application to use bind variables. This may involve redesigning the application to use set operations instead of individual row operations. It may involve compiler flags to allow cursor sharing. It may involve changing the location of a parse call from within a loop to before the loop so the parse call is made once; instead of once per execution. Any one or several of these options may be involved. The next case study shows how to determine the current level of cursor utilization.

If this is a third party application, do not despair. The database parameter *cursor_sharing* can be set to FORCE or SIMILAR instead of the default value of EXACT. This allows the cost based optimizer to use the execution plan of an already parsed statement when the statement would be identical other than for the literal values. In other words, if the application were using bind variables, these statements would look the same.

The *cursor_sharing* parameter can have a negative performance impact in some situations, such as when an application uses stored outlines or in decision support systems (DSS). Be sure to read and test thoroughly, before implementing this parameter in a production environment.

Case #2. Network Capacity Bottleneck

When a user opens a problem report stating the database is slow, it is essential to gather *v$* data as soon as possible to avoid having to tell the user that a problem could not be found and they should call back if things get worse again. One way to do this is to look at the active sessions and see what the user is waiting for.

The *active_session_waits.sql* script shows the session-level wait statistics for the sessions that are currently active. It is best to run this a number of times in a row in order to spot the recurring sessions that keep showing up.

🖫 active_session_waits.sql

```
-- ****************************************************
-- Copyright © 2003 by Rampant TechPress
-- This script is free for non-commercial purposes
-- with no warranties.  Use at your own risk.
--
-- To license this script for a commercial purpose,
-- contact info@rampant.cc
-- ****************************************************

/* active_session_waits.sql */

column EVENT      format a24
column STATE      format a24
column USERNAME   format a10
column SID        format 9999
column TIME       format 9999
column SEC        format 9999
column SERIAL#    format 999999
column WAIT_TIME  format 99 HEAD TIME

select
   b.SID,
   a.SERIAL#,
```

```
   a.USERNAME,
   b.EVENT,
   b.WAIT_TIME TIME,
   b.STATE,
   b.SECONDS_IN_WAIT SEC
from
   V$SESSION a,
   V$SESSION_WAIT b
where
   a.USERNAME is not null
and
   b.SID = a.SID
order by
   b.WAIT_TIME desc;
```

This script produces output like this sample case:

```
Oracle@prod> @active_session_waits.sql

 SID SERIAL# USERNAME EVENT                      TIME STATE                SEC
 --- ------- -------- ------------------------   ---- ------------------   ---
 191   22140 FIRST    db file sequential read       0 WAITING                0
 340   61830 FIRST    null event                   -1 WAITED KNOWN TIME      0
 400   32039 ORACLE   null event                   -1 WAITED KNOWN TIME      0
```

First of all, since this is Oracle case was run on version 9.2.0.3, one of the bugs mentioned earlier is showing up. The "null event" waits have no value and cannot provide information on what the bottleneck or resource constraint is. An upgrade is planned, but the user needs this performance issue resolved. Therefore, ignoring the null events for the time being is necessary even though they are most likely significant.

Later, the 10046 trace will be used to to get more information on sessions. For now though, the focus will be on the "db file sequential read." This means that this process is most likely performing an index scan.

It would be helpful to see what index is being read, so run *specific_session_waits.sql.*

```
-- **************************************************
-- Copyright © 2003 by Rampant TechPress
-- This script is free for non-commercial purposes
-- with no warranties.  Use at your own risk.
--
-- To license this script for a commercial purpose,
-- contact info@rampant.cc
-- **************************************************

/* specific_session_waits.sql */
column P1      format 999999
column P2      format 999999
column P3      format 999
column P1TEXT  format a10
column P2TEXT  format a8
column P3TEXT  format a8

select
   SID,
   EVENT,
   P1TEXT,
   P1,
   P2TEXT,
   P2,
   P3TEXT,
   P3
from
   V$SESSION_WAIT
where
   SID in (&sid);
```

```
Oracle@prod> @specific_session_waits.sql
Enter value for sid: 191

SID EVENT                         P1TEXT            P1 P2TEXT  P2
--- ----------------------------- --------- ---------- ------ ---
191 SQL*Net message from client   driver id 1650815232 #bytes   1
```

Does this mean the index being read is actually located somewhere else (SQL*Net)? No, it just means that by the time the script name had been typed and executed, the session reading the index had finished. It was probably in the process of communicating with the client session and getting the next command to run. When this happens frequently, the user's session may be bottlenecking on the network communication. Now that the WHAT is known, the question becomes WHY? It is possible to monitor the frequency of this wait event showing up in *v$session_wait*. When it becomes more prevalent, consider the possibility that network bandwidth may be lacking.

This can be fixed in two main ways. First, in the "throw more money at it" category, upgrade the network infrastructure. Switches, cable and network cards are all targets, and the network group will need to be consulted to help identify where the biggest bottleneck is.

Another approach is to look at how the application is using the network and investigate ways of reducing the load. One way of reducing network traffic is to eliminate excess parsing. Every parse requires at least one round-trip between the application server, or client server in a 2-tier configuration, and the database server. If a statement is parsed 100,000 times more than needed, there is a lot of traffic on the network that is not adding any value to the business.

In many cases, changing a compiler flag, and recompiling the application or increasing the number of cursors will help to reduce the unnecessary parses. There are a couple of things the DBA can change in the database configuration that can help reduce excessive parsing.

The script *cursor_usage.sql* is one way to determine whether the parse load on the database could be reduced through better cache utilization. Most of the time, this approach makes the business happier since it makes better use of resources. Also, this approach allows delaying the hardware upgrade solution to a time when it will be truly needed.

One should also try diagnosing network performance with the usual tools like *ping*, *traceroute*, *nslookup*, *spray* and *netstat*. Some network engineers monitor only capacity of the line, not the actual throughput. It is important to thoroughly test the line because network problems can be very difficult to diagnose and address.

💾 cursor_usage.sql

```
--  ***************************************************
-- Copyright © 2003 by Rampant TechPress
-- This script is free for non-commercial purposes
-- with no warranties.  Use at your own risk.
--
-- To license this script for a commercial purpose,
-- contact info@rampant.cc
--  ***************************************************

/* cursor_usage.sql */
select
  'session_cached_cursors'  parameter,
  lpad(value, 5)  value,
  decode(value, 0, '  n/a', to_char(100 * used / value, '990') ||
'%')  usage
from
  ( select
      max(s.value)  used
    from
      sys.v_$statname  n,
      sys.v_$sesstat  s
    where
      n.name = 'session cursor cache count' and
      s.statistic# = n.statistic#
  ),
  ( select
      value
    from
      sys.v_$parameter
    where
      name = 'session_cached_cursors'
  )
union all
select
  'open_cursors',
  lpad(value, 5),
  to_char(100 * used / value,  '990') || '%'
from
  ( select
      max(sum(s.value))  used
    from
      sys.v_$statname  n,
      sys.v_$sesstat  s
    where
      n.name in ('opened cursors current', 'session cursor cache
count') and
```

```
          s.statistic# = n.statistic#
     group by
          s.sid
  ),
  ( select
        value
     from
        sys.v_$parameter
     where
        name = 'open_cursors'
  );
```

```
SQL> @cursor_usage

PARAMETER               VALUE USAGE
--------------------- ----- -----
session_cached_cursors    20    0%
open_cursors             255    4%
```

As evidenced by the output, the existing 255 cursors that are available are only being used 4% of the time, so increasing that will not reduce the parsing. Since *session_cached_cursors* does not appear to be used, it probably set high enough already.

Beyond reducing parsing, another way to reduce network traffic is to investigate the efficiency of the queries. If an application is retrieving 100,000 rows and then displaying only the 10 rows with a particular value, it is possible to eliminate 99,990 rows from the network every time that function is executed.

Standard disclaimer: Seek to imitate the offending behavior in the test system first. Then test the proposed corrections before trying them in a live production environment.

Case #3. Storage Capacity Restrictions

Another example of the wait interface in action can be seen in this example of an I/O bottleneck.

Previously *iostat* and other operating system utilities were mentioned. Being a proactive DBA, iostat was run at 2-second intervals for a period of time, and the output saved to a file for a baseline measurement. This was done during the time the users classified as "normal," meaning the system did not seem abnormally slow or workload unusually light. By using the *grep* command to filter out a single key or representative device along with a spreadsheet, the last lines of the report and analysis look like Figure 5.4.

Device:	tps	Blk_read/s	Blk_wrtn/s	Blk_read	Blk_wrtn
dev3-0	10	0	180	0	360
dev3-0	4.5	0	84	0	168
dev3-0	4.5	0	84	0	168
dev3-0	5.5	0	96	0	192
dev3-0	9	0	168	0	336
dev3-0	5.5	0	96	0	192
dev3-0	4.5	0	84	0	168
dev3-0	9	0	168	0	336
dev3-0	5.5	0	96	0	192
dev3-0	4.5	0	84	0	168
dev3-0	7	0	107	0	214
dev3-0	9	0	168	0	336
dev3-0	4.5	0	84	0	168
dev3-0	7	12	96	24	192
dev3-0	9	0	168	0	336
MAX	247	3,184	4,096	6,368	8,192
AVG	36	364	183	727	367

Figure 5.4 – *Baseline iostat report*

For this measurement period, there was an average of 727 blocks read and 367 blocks written per 2-second interval. When a call about slowness issues comes in, it is possible to quickly determine how much I/O is being done compared to the baseline. The analysis of the *iostat* that was run during a reported performance problem is shown in Figure 5.5. This run was done with a 1 second interval to closely monitor the system for a few minutes.

Oracle Wait Event Tuning

Device:	tps	Blk_read/s	Blk_wrtn/s	Blk_read	Blk_wrtn
dev3-0	145.28	4773.58	2571.7	5060	2726
dev3-0	76	3264	234	3264	234
dev3-0	163	11672	138	11672	138
dev3-0	168	6352	0	6352	0
dev3-0	102	3848	6584	3848	6584
dev3-0	143	10560	126	10560	126
dev3-0	157	1776	5594	1776	5594
dev3-0	113.08	6960.75	134.58	7448	144
dev3-0	198	8216	8240	8216	8240
dev3-0	216	10640	48	10640	48
dev3-0	198	6840	12056	6840	12056
MAX	**285**	**12,536**	**12,720**	**12,536**	**12,720**
AVG	**117**	**4,610**	**3,372**	**4,621**	**3,375**

Figure 5.5 – *Analysis of a busy iostat report*

The average for blocks read and written per second is significantly higher on this device than it was during the baseline period. In fact, the highest number of read and writes per second in the baseline (3,184 & 4,096) are close to the average during the performance problem (4,610 & 3,372).

The question that must now be investigated is whether the I/O bottleneck is causing the performance problems the users are seeing, or if it is only symptomatic of the problem. To put it another way, the users could be seeing slowness because something in the storage system changed. For example, a change from RAID 1+0 to RAID 5 might speed up reads, but slow down writes. Or, given the reads and writes are of a similar magnitude in the baseline as well as in the busy measurements, some other operation could be suspected of causing a lot of extra operations on this device.

To answer that question, it will be necessary to get into the database and investigate who is using most I/O operations, and what type of response time they are seeing. The *start_system_events.sql,* *finish_system_events.sql* and *difference_system_events.sql* scripts may be useful in identifying what events are waiting most often.

The output below is from *difference_system_events.sql* with a twist. Since the results of the *iostat* indicate a high volume of activity, the sort order can be changed to show the top number of waits instead of total time or average wait.

EVENT	WAITS	TIMEOUTS	TIME WAITED	AVG WAIT
db file scattered read	561	0	14283	0
db file sequential read	295	0	1665	0
rdbms ipc message	216	136	28787	0
log file parallel write	74	74	0	0
PL/SQL lock timer	73	73	3735	0
buffer busy waits	60	19	2614	0
SQL*Net message from client	51	0	205862	22

For the interval between the start and finish scripts being run, which was approximately the same time period that *iostat* was running, the db file scattered read and db file sequential read events were the most common events. Even though the average wait for these events is reported as 0, it is important to remember that the time in the TIME WAITED column is reported in centiseconds.

Seeing a measurable average wait above 20 milliseconds would not be expected, even for low performance I/O systems. Some storage area network vendors predict 3 milliseconds or less(*). As a representative for one vendor once explained that if they saw I/O response times of 30 milliseconds, it would be considered a major disaster, which would get their 24x7 attention until it was resolved.

Therefore, even in an I/O problem of 10-20 milliseconds, the average time per wait could still show up as less than 2 centiseconds. This is not to say that a high number of waits indicates a problem. It just means that based on other information available, namely *iostat* numbers, the quantity of db file scattered read and db file sequential read events deserve a bit more attention than the 0 centisecond average wait would normally get.

The next stop then would be to see how the database is performing on all of its I/O operations. A script called *io_report_volume.sql* can help here. Depending on the number of files in the system, it may be helpful to add a condition to the where clause restricting this to the top 10 rows, or something manageable.

io_report_volume.sql

```
-- *************************************************
-- Copyright © 2003 by Rampant TechPress
-- This script is free for non-commercial purposes
-- with no warranties.  Use at your own risk.
--
-- To license this script for a commercial purpose,
-- contact info@rampant.cc
-- *************************************************

/* io_report_volume.sql */
column FILE_NAME        format a30
column PHYRDS           format 999,999
column PHYWRTS          format 999,999
column READTIM          format 999,999
column "READ AVG (ms)"  format 999.99
column "TOTAL I/O"      format 999,999

select
   FILE_NAME,
   PHYRDS,
   READTIM,
   PHYWRTS,
   READTIM / (PHYRDS + 1) "READ AVG (ms)",
   PHYRDS + PHYWRTS "TOTAL I/O"

from
   V$FILESTAT a,
   DBA_DATA_FILES b

where
   a.FILE# = b.FILE_ID
```

```
order by
   6 DESC;
```

FILE_NAME	PHYRDS	READTIM	PHYWRTS	READ (ms)	TOTAL I/O
/oradata/TOY/data02.dbf	5,666	13,274	1	2.34	5,667
/oradata/TOY/data01.dbf	5,602	11,051	7	1.97	5,609
/oradata/TOY/system01.dbf	2,458	3,066	321	1.25	2,779
/oradata/TOY/users02.dbf	639	539	267	.84	906
/oradata/TOY/temp01.dbf	164	6	203	.04	367
/oradata/TOY/rbs01.dbf	30	37	180	1.19	210
/oradata/TOY/users01.dbf	72	69	95	.95	167
/oradata/TOY/index01.dbf	13	16	1	1.14	14
/oradata/TOY/tools01.dbf	7	2	1	.25	8
/oradata/TOY/rcvcat01.dbf	3	0	1	.00	4

There has been some heavy read activity going on in the data01.dbf and data02.dbf datafiles. In this case, it would be easy to guess that these files probably belong to the DATA tablespace. However, it is always better to be sure since the file might belong to the two different tablespaces, DATA01 and DATA02. Running *find_tbs.sql* will help determine what tablespace a given file belongs to.

🖫 find_tbs.sql

```
--  ****************************************************
-- Copyright © 2003 by Rampant TechPress
-- This script is free for non-commercial purposes
-- with no warranties.  Use at your own risk.
--
-- To license this script for a commercial purpose,
-- contact info@rampant.cc
--  ****************************************************

/* find_tbs.sql */
-- Find the name of a tablespace that
-- a particular datafile belongs to.
-- Prompts user for at least a partial file name.

column TABLESPACE_NAME format a15
column FILE_NAME       format a30
column STATUS          format a10

select
   TABLESPACE_NAME,
   FILE_NAME,
   STATUS
```

Oracle Wait Event Tuning

```
from
   DBA_DATA_FILES
where
   FILE_NAME like '%&partial_file_name%'
order by
   FILE_NAME;
```

```
SQL> @find_tbs
Enter value for partial_file_name: data0
old    8:     FILE_NAME like '%&partial_file_name%'
new    8:     FILE_NAME like '%data0%'

TABLESPACE_NAME FILE_NAME                         STATUS
--------------- --------------------------------- ----------
DATA01          /oradata/TOY/data01.dbf           AVAILABLE
DATA01          /oradata/TOY/data02.dbf           AVAILABLE
```

Now it is known for certain that these two "hot" datafiles belong to the DATA tablespace. From here, it is time to look at the top sessions and see what SQL they are running and if the number of reads from these files can be reduced.

session_event_users.sql is run to list users currently waiting, as any session contributing to the large quantity of physical reads will probably be doing.

```
SQL> @session_event_users
```

USERNAME	SID	EVENT	TOTAL WAITS	TOTAL TIME OUTS	TIME WAITED	AVG WAIT	MAX WAIT	TIME WAITED MICRO
ORACLE	11	SQL*Net message from	109	0	230085	2111	66743	2300847746
WEBBER	12	library cache pin	2	0	148	74	137	1477676
WEBBER	16	library cache pin	3	0	166	55	154	1659908
WEBBER	15	library cache pin	3	0	165	55	153	1647897
WEBBER	19	library cache pin	3	0	166	55	154	1661282
WEBBER	12	buffer busy waits	821	52	32920	40	154	329203732
WEBBER	19	buffer busy waits	736	49	27926	38	135	279256344
WEBBER	16	buffer busy waits	771	57	29498	38	191	294977569
WEBBER	9	buffer busy waits	854	42	31971	37	161	319710954
WEBBER	8	buffer busy waits	841	38	30360	36	163	303600211
WEBBER	15	buffer busy waits	771	46	28109	36	145	281092677
WEBBER	13	buffer busy waits	837	42	30460	36	119	304600108

The user WEBBER is likely a good candidate for further examination. The sessions with the buffer busy waits have significantly more wait events and timeouts; therefore, run *show_session_sql.sql* a couple of them to see what SQL is being executed.

```
SQL> @show_session_sql
Enter value for sid: 12
old  12:            SID = '&sid')
new  12:            SID = '12')

SQL_TEXT
-------------------------------------------------------------
SELECT count(*) from   hits where  upper(area) != 'a'

SQL> /
Enter value for sid: 19
old  12:            SID = '&sid')
new  12:            SID = '19')

SQL_TEXT
-------------------------------------------------------------
SELECT count(*) from   hits where  upper(area) != 'a'
```

By running this a couple of times for a few of the session identifiers noticed previously, the SQL statement that these sessions are running can be identified. In this case, it looks like several sessions are running the same thing. In all likelihood a report was kicked off multiple times. Also, notice that the condition in the where clause is using literal values instead of bind variables.

Multiple approaches to solving the current problem have been presented. One is to investigate why multiple copies of the same statement were being executed by different sessions and work on finding a way to reduce the number of sessions doing the same work. If that is not possible or unsuccessful, other options must be investigated This could include database changes like materialized views; application redesign ideas like query tuning, bind variable usage or even business process review to see if there are changes that could make the business procedures more efficient, productive and more database efficient.

Conclusion

This chapter started with an overview about the Wait Interface, which was a review of the discussion in Chapter 2. After the overview, the rest of the chapter demonstrated ways that can be used to apply the Wait Interface to practical tuning problems. This demonstration was done through three case study examples that demonstrated step-by-step how to approach various tuning problems. This chapter also included a number of scripts that can be used to apply these steps to real life performance tuning issues.

In the next chapter, the same process will be used to explain and demonstrate how to use event 10046 tracing to solve performance problems.

Using 10046 Tracing

Defining 10046 Tracing

Earlier 10046 Tracing was introduced as a way to obtain information about the execution of jobs running in the database. This chapter will refresh that information, and then look at case studies to demonstrate ways to identify sessions to trace, tracing them, and then analyzing the output in a number of ways.

Event 10046 enables the collection of extended SQL trace information. In this chapter, more challenging examples of gathering and analyzing extended SQL trace information will be examined.

The example used earlier was a level 1 trace, which included neither bind variable nor wait information. In this chapter, level 12 trace information will be examined exclusively. This includes both bind variable data as well as wait information. A level 12 trace allows the use of data collected by the Wait Interface to analyze and determine what the biggest contributors to the jobs response time are.

Use the Wait Interface to determine what the biggest contributors to the jobs response time are.

Identification of the biggest response time contributor is key because the best hope of tuning a slow process lies in identifying where the largest amount of time is spend and finding ways to reduce that time.

Setting-up for 10046 tracing

To successfully trace a session use the parameter settings *timed_statistics* and *max_dump_file_size*. The *tracefile_identifier* parameter can be used to add a keyword to the name of trace files for a given session for easier identification. There are a number of scripts that are going to be used in this chapter to demonstrate ways to quickly identify the information required to trace a specific session.

Some of the scripts introduced previously will be widely used in this chapter; they include *session_identification.sql, prepare_current_session.sql,* and *prepare_other_session.sql.* Additional scripts will be introduced throughout with examples and all scripts are available for download from the Code Depot. Using the trace file generated by Event 10046, a demonstration will be provided on how to perform manual trace file analysis in addition to demonstrations of other tools that can be used to determine the root cause of a slowness issue.

Once the database is set-up with the appropriate parameters for tracing, and scripts or the syntax for commands is available and understood, then it is time for the most important preparatory step, knowing what to trace and how long to trace. These are critical *planning* steps. Failing to plan what session is going to be traced and how long to trace may result in a trace file that does not contain the desired data. Consider that even though the intended session is the one being traced, if the trace is started too soon before the questionable process executes, then any user interaction will show up in the trace file and may mask the true bottleneck. Tracing at the right time, but the wrong session has obvious implications. Tracing too short of a time frame may not give enough information about the process to know where to make improvements.

The best plan for tracing is to include trace functionality in the application. If a particular report is slow, have the developers include an environment setting script like *prepare_current_session.sql.* This allows tracing to start immediately before the report processing starts and stop immediately afterwards. The trace file will not have any extraneous data from user "processing" time like coffee breaks, phone calls, or other tasks that could delay stopping the tracing activity as soon as the report or process finishes.

Unfortunately, it will not always be possible to modify program code to enable tracing, so some alternative options will be demonstrated in the following Case Studies. Each Case Study wil start with a scenario, and use it to demonstrate how to tune performance the Wait Interface way using event 10046 to gather extended SQL trace statistics.

Case Study #1 – High CPU Utilization

A user calls and reports that the system is slow. First, attempt to narrow the scope of the problem by investigating whether this is impacting all users of the application, all portions of the application, or all applications. Log in and analyze the status of this database, the database server, and either the application server or the middleware server.

Figure 6.1 is an example of the output from the UNIX operating system command *top* followed by the *ps* command. There is a process that is using almost 98% of the CPU time. This process is running against the *TOY* instance on this server. A second *ps* command is used to learn that the parent process that launched this process is *sqlplus,* and its process id is 22013. The process id (PID) for the high CPU process is 22014. This information will be used Now this information will be used to dig into the database to learn more about this process.

```
12:19am  up 32 days,  1:24,  3 users,  load average: 0.99, 1.04, 1.34
86 processes: 84 sleeping, 2 running, 0 zombie, 0 stopped
CPU states: 98.8% user,  1.1% system,  0.0% nice,  0.0% idle
Mem:   126804K av,  124060K used,    2744K free,      0K shrd,   10432K buff
Swap: 1020088K av,  126684K used,  893404K free                 91236K cached

  PID USER     PRI  NI  SIZE  RSS SHARE STAT %CPU %MEM    TIME COMMAND
22014 oracle    25   0 21676  21M 19820 R    97.8 17.0    3:19 oracle
22005 oracle    16   0  1024 1024   792 R     2.1  0.8    0:09 top
    1 root      15   0   464  420   400 S     0.0  0.3    0:04 init
    2 root      15   0     0    0     0 SW    0.0  0.0    0:00 keventd
    3 root      15   0     0    0     0 SW    0.0  0.0    0:00 kapmd
    4 root      34  19     0    0     0 SWN   0.0  0.0    0:00 ksoftirqd_CPU0
    5 root      15   0     0    0     0 SW    0.0  0.0    1:27 kswapd
    6 root      15   0     0    0     0 SW    0.0  0.0    0:00 bdflush
    7 root      15   0     0    0     0 SW    0.0  0.0    0:01 kupdated
    8 root      25   0     0    0     0 SW    0.0  0.0    0:00 mdrecoveryd
   14 root      15   0     0    0     0 SW    0.0  0.0    0:25 kjournald
   84 root      15   0     0    0     0 SW    0.0  0.0    0:00 khubd
  221 root      15   0     0    0     0 SW    0.0  0.0    0:00 kjournald
  222 root      15   0     0    0     0 SW    0.0  0.0    0:00 kjournald
  223 root      15   0     0    0     0 SW    0.0  0.0   22:04 kjournald
  224 root      15   0     0    0     0 SW    0.0  0.0    0:03 kjournald
  593 root      15   0   548  496   480 S     0.0  0.3    0:01 syslogd
[oracle@matthew book]$ ps -ef | grep 22014
oracle   22014 22013 90 00:16 ?         00:03:32 oracleTOY (DESCRIPTION=(LOCAL=YE
oracle   22019 21635  0 00:20 pts/1     00:00:00 grep 22014
[oracle@matthew book]$
[oracle@matthew book]$ ps -ef | grep 22013
oracle   22013 21796  0 00:16 pts/4     00:00:00 sqlplus
oracle   22014 22013 94 00:16 ?         00:07:02 oracleTOY (DESCRIPTION=(LOCAL=YE
oracle   22021 21635  0 00:23 pts/1     00:00:00 grep 22013
```

Figure 6.1 – *top of Database Server*

Use the process id (PID) obtained in the above manner to
discover which user in the database is making the system work so
hard. The following script, *find_db_user.sql*, will prompt for a
UNIX process id and will provide the information that will be
required later about the user in order to do further tuning with
extended SQL tracing. Figure 6.2 shows the output from the
sample run of this script.

💾 *find_db_user.sql*

```
-- *******************************************************
-- Copyright © 2003 by Rampant TechPress
-- This script is free for non-commercial purposes
-- with no warranties.  Use at your own risk.
--
-- To license this script for a commercial purpose,
-- contact info@rampant.cc
```

```
-- *****************************************************
column spid format 999999
column sid format 99999
column serial# format 99999
column username format a15

accept unix_pid prompt 'Enter the UNIX process ID: '

select
   spid,
   sid,
   a.serial#,
   a.username "User in DB",
   b.username "User in OS"
from
   v$session a, v$process b
where
   paddr = addr
and
   spid = '&unix_pid';
```

```
SQL> @find_db_user
Enter the UNIX process ID: 22014
old  12:    SPID = '&UNIX_PID'
new  12:    SPID = '22014'

SPID       SID SERIAL# User in DB      User in OS
--------  ------ ------- --------------- ------------
22014        8    5205 KEVIN           oracle
```

Figure 6.2 – *Finding database user information*

By using *top,* it is quickly discovered that there is a process that is nearly maxing out a CPU. With the *ps* command it is discovered that the user was local (from the LOCAL=YE in the *ps* output) and was running SQL*plus.

The *find_db_user.sql* script quickly provided the username of the responsible person for this process. It is KEVIN, the database sid is 8, and the serial# is 5205. These two numbers will be used to enable tracing for this session. However, first use *show_session_sql.sql* to see what SQL this session is currently executing.

```
-- ***************************************************
-- Copyright © 2003 by Rampant TechPress
-- This script is free for non-commercial purposes
-- with no warranties.  Use at your own risk.
--
-- To license this script for a commercial purpose,
-- contact info@rampant.cc
-- ***************************************************

/* show_session_sql.sql */
select
   sql_text
from
   v$sqltext
where
   hash_value in (
      select
         sql_hash_value
      from
         v$session
      where
         sid = '&sid')
order by
   piece;
```

The output from this script is shown in Figure 6.3.

```
SQL> @show_session_sql.sql
Enter value for sid: 8
old   12:         SID = '&sid')
new   12:         SID = '8')

SQL_TEXT
-----------------------------------------------------------------
select count(*) X from kill_cpu connect by n > prior n start with n
= 1
```

Figure 6.3 – *Show SQL for a given session id (sid)*

This shows what this session is executing right at the moment. Now, if tracing is enabled for this session, it can be determined whether this session is the cause of the problem or only a contributor. This script could be run repeatedly to see what SQL appears most often. However, this is rather subjective and may not provide the same level of accuracy that a 10046 trace will.

The results of *find_db_user.sql* shown in Figure 6.2, show that the sid and serial# are, 8 and 5205 respectively. Use the script *trace_other_12.sql* to set *timed_statistics* and *max_dump_file_size* and turn on tracing. Figure 6.4 below shows the output and the command to stop tracing after a little over two minutes.

The SQL*Plus command prompt has a time stamp. This is a handy way to track how long different tasks take. By issuing the command *set time on* at an SQL*Plus prompt, the timestamp is part of the prompt. Likewise, the command *set timing on* will provide information on the duration of a given command once it finishes.

🖫 *trace_other_12.sql*

```
--  **************************************************
--  Copyright © 2003 by Rampant TechPress
--  This script is free for non-commercial purposes
--  with no warranties.  Use at your own risk.
--
--  To license this script for a commercial purpose,
--  contact info@rampant.cc
--  **************************************************

/* trace_other_12.sql */
--  This script will make sure timed statistics
--     and max_dump_file_size are set correctly in
--     preparation for tracing a specific session.
--     Then this script will start level 12 tracing

accept sid prompt 'Enter the SID: '
accept serial prompt 'Enter the SERIAL#: '

execute sys.dbms_system.set_bool_param_in_session (&sid, &serial,
'timed_statistics', TRUE);

execute .dbms_system.set_int_param_in_session (&sid, &serial,
'max_dump_file_size', 2000000000);

execute dbms_support.start_trace_in_session (&sid, &serial,
waits=>TRUE, binds=>TRUE);
```

```
19:54:40 SQL> &trace_other_12
Enter the SID: 8
Enter the SERIAL#:5205

PL/SQL procedure successfully completed.

PL/SQL procedure successfully completed.

PL/SQL procedure successfully completed.

19:57:03 SQL> execute DBMS_SUPPORT.STOP_TRACE_IN_SESSION (&SID,
&SERIAL);

PL/SQL procedure successfully completed.
```

Figure 6.4 – *Tracing a user's session*

The trace file that was produced is over 40 million lines long. To gain a better understanding of what this session, some basic analysis can be performed using simple UNIX operating system commands.

The first step is to determine how many of those events were WAIT events rather than PARSE, EXEC or FETCH events were. There were 19,677 WAIT events, over 13 million EXEC events, 0 PARSE events and over 13 million FETCH events. In fact, the number of FETCH events matches the number of EXEC events. The 0 parses probably reflect the fact that all the SQL statements being used by this process had already been parsed before tracing began. However, it is a good indicator that the problems are not due to excessive parsing. Now it is time to determine what the primary WAIT events were. Opening the trace file in a text editor is probably not a good idea since the file is roughly 2 GBs and it will either crash the editor or tie up the session for a long time. A better way would be to *cat* the file with *grep* and *head* to look at the first handful of events in order to get a feel for the types of WAIT events. Figure 6.5 shows these commands along with the first handful of lines of WAIT events.

```
[oracle@matthew udump]$ cat toy_ora_16536.trc | wc -1 40144396
[oracle@matthew udump]$ cat toy_ora_16536.trc | grep WAIT | wc -1 19677
[oracle@matthew udump]$ cat toy_ora_16536.trc | grep EXEC | wc -1 13374884
[oracle@matthew udump]$ cat toy_ora_16536.trc | grep PARSE | wc -1 0
[oracle@matthew udump]$ cat toy_ora_16536.trc | grep FETCH | wc -1 13374884
[oracle@matthew udump]$ cat toy_ora_16536.trc | grep WAIT | head -20
WAIT #4: nam='latch free' ela= 14 p1=1406391244 p2=97 p3=0
WAIT #4: nam='latch free' ela= 138701 p1=1406391244 p2=97 p3=1
WAIT #10: nam='latch free' ela= 14 p1=1406391244 p2=97 p3=0
WAIT #10: nam='latch free' ela= 144988 p1=1406391244 p2=97 p3=1
WAIT #11: nam='latch free' ela= 145928 p1=1412453816 p2=156 p3=0
WAIT #8: nam='latch free' ela= 146014 p1=1412453816 p2=156 p3=0
WAIT #6: nam='latch free' ela= 17 p1=1406390972 p2=97 p3=0
WAIT #6: nam='latch free' ela= 141897 p1=1406390972 p2=97 p3=1
WAIT #5: nam='latch free' ela= 16 p1=1406391244 p2=97 p3=0
WAIT #5: nam='latch free' ela= 146022 p1=1406391244 p2=97 p3=1
WAIT #6: nam='latch free' ela= 15 p1=1406390972 p2=97 p3=0
WAIT #6: nam='latch free' ela= 144359 p1=1406390972 p2=97 p3=1
WAIT #11: nam='latch free' ela= 16 p1=1406390972 p2=97 p3=0
WAIT #11: nam='latch free' ela= 144175 p1=1406390972 p2=97 p3=1
WAIT #10: nam='latch free' ela= 146236 p1=1412453816 p2=156 p3=0
WAIT #10: nam='latch free' ela= 146207 p1=1412453816 p2=156 p3=1
WAIT #8: nam='latch free' ela= 146145 p1=1412453816 p2=156 p3=0
```

Figure 6.5 – *Manual Trace File Analysis*

Notice that the only WAIT event seen here is for latch free. Additional analysis of this file will reveal that latch free is the only WAIT event. While latch free could indicate an excessive parsing problem, the earlier analysis showing 0 parse events tends to indicate that is not the problem.

One way to analyze trace files manually would be to write a program in Perl or a similar language. Since the focus of this book it not on writing Perl script, this option is left up to the reader to pursue if desired. The Trace Analyzer is another way to dig deeper into the file to identify and isolate the cause for this problem. Several sections of the report generated by running *trcanlzr.sql* against this trace file will be shown in the next couple of figures.

```
WAITED_NON-IDLE_TIME...: 454.36 SECS
WAITED_IDLE_TIME.......: 0.00


*******************************************************************

NUMBER_OF_CURSORS......: 10 (USER), 0 (INTERNAL <SYS>), 10 (TOTAL)
UNIQUE_SQL.............: 10 (USER), 0 (INTERNAL <SYS>), 10 (TOTAL)

*******************************************************************
```

Figure 6.6 – *Trace Analyzer Summary Information*

Figure 6.6 displays part of the summary information in the header section of the Trace Analyzer report. The summary of idle vs. non-idle can be potentially misleading. Remember the discussion earlier about the importance of setting the scope of the tracing? Well, here is one place that will be impacted if the scope is not set correctly. Excessive values in the WAITED_IDLE_TIME section of this report would be seen. If tracing is properly scoped, WAITED_IDLE_TIME could represent SQL*Net waits accumulating due to a network configuration problem. Additional statistics to check in this section of the report are the number of cursors and the number of unique SQL statements. If there are more cursors than unique SQL, then try and determine why they are not sharing more.

In the next section of the report, shown in Figure 6.7, is a list of the top SQL statements.

```
TOP SQL (SUMMARY OF CPU, ELAPSED AND WAITS PER TOP EXPENSIVE CURSOR)
===================================================================

cursor user                                      non-idle      idle
id     id   command type   count     cpu top elapsed top  waits top waits top
------ ---- ------------   -------  ------- --- ------- ---  -------- --- ----- ---
7      31   select         563232 1355.14 1  2722.26 1     96.68 1   0.00 1
10     31   select         563230  881.14 2  1730.39 2     69.67 2   0.00
8      31   select         563232  282.29 3   558.43 3     50.42 3   0.00 2
2      31   select         563232  281.76 4   536.30 5     28.56     0.00
4      31   select         563232  281.29 5   517.01        25.50     0.00
6      31   select         563232  274.48      536.70 4     44.65 5   0.00
9      31   select         563231  276.80      536.01        45.82 4   0.00 5
1      31   select         563232  277.14      522.36        28.10     0.00 3
5      31   select         563232  279.13      518.76        23.61     0.00 4
```

Figure 6.7 – *Trace Analyzer Top SQL Summary*

Oracle Wait Event Tuning

The full text of the statement is not shown here, however what is shown is whether it is a *select, insert, update* or *delete* statement.

Please notice that the four main columns *cpu, elapsed, non-idle waits* and *idle waits* all have a small column called *top* immediately to their right. The *top* column shows the ordinal number that represents the rank of that statement or cursor. In this case, the top cursor in terms of all four categories is number 7. This statement consumed nearly twice the CPU time than the next statement, 1355 compared to 881. Another important column here is the count column which allows the viewing of how many times each statement has been run. In looking at the sample, notice that each of these statements executed more than 500,000 times during the time of the tracing. Without knowledge of how the application is intended to work, a DBA might not know whether or not this is a reasonable number of executions. However, a good Developer would have a good idea. This information might mean that a loop was designed wrong. Instead of running 50 times for 1000 rows, it is actually running 500 times for 1000 rows. The best performing SQL statement is one that does not get executed.

Figure 6.8 shows the Top Waits by User in this Trace Analyzer report.

```
********************************************************************
SUMMARY OF WAITS BY USER (INTERNAL LAST) AND NON-RECURSIVE/RECURSIVE
====================================================================

WAITS FOR ALL RECURSIVE STATEMENTS FOR USER 31 (KEVIN)

Event                                     Times    Count   Max.   Total
Waited on                                 Waited Zero Time  Wait  Waited
----------------------------------------  ------ --------- -----  -------
latch free (156 library cache)..........    1546        0  0.44   225.76
latch free (097 cache buffers chains)...    2328        0  0.29   168.48
latch free (157 library cache pin)......     413        0  0.29    60.13
----------------------------------------  ------ --------- -----  -------
total...................................    4287        0  0.44   454.36

non-idle waits..........................    4287        0  0.44   454.36
idle waits..............................       0        0  0.00     0.00

********************************************************************
```

Figure 6.8 – *Trace Analyzer Top Waits by User*

Figure 6.5 showed a selection of the raw trace file WAIT events, which showed the latch free as the dominant WAIT event. Figure 6.8 shows the breakdown of what those latch free events were for. Library cache caused 1546 WAIT events. Cache buffers chains caused 2328 WAIT events and library cache pins caused 413 WAIT events. Notice that the latch free events for library cache represented almost 50% of the time waited. This is displayed in the right most column of Figure 6.8 in which the time waited is shown as 225.76 seconds and the total time is 454.36 seconds. In order to reduce the amount of time this process is waiting, the biggest impact would be realized by reducing the time that is spent waiting for library cache latch free events.

So in conclusion, by using a 10046 trace and the Trace Analyzer tool from Oracle, it was possible to establish that there are at least two areas to look at for improvement:

- Reducing number of executions
- Reducing contention for the library cache latch

Case #2 – Excessive Use of Single Row Operations

In this scenario, the operators were responsible for monitoring the process of a batch process that runs daily. They noticed that the process often takes 10-12 hours and many times fails with the ORA-01555 error - snapshot too old, and the job then requires restarting. The decision was made to use a 10046 trace in order to see what can be done to improve performance and reduce the occurrence of the ORA-01555 error.

After quick research, it was discovered that the job caused an excessive amount of growth in the rollback segment tablespace. This growth had caused failure to extend messages previously, so a job had been scheduled to shrink the rollback segments periodically to avoid this problem. Unfortunately, when the shrink job ran during the batch job, it caused the ORA-01555 that the operators reported. The OPTIMAL setting could also trigger this problem so it had been omitted from the CREATE ROLLBACK SEGMENT statement. So to reduce the occurrences of the ORA-01555, causing the job to fail, the rollback segment needs to be able to grow sufficiently to accommodate the job. After the job is complete, the shrink job can be run to ensure rollback segments are sized correctly for the daytime operations.

As mentioned before, the decision was made to use the event 10046 to gather extended SQL trace data. Due to the way the job runs, there is not an easy way to include the commands to prepare the environment and start tracing within the program. Consequently, it will be necessary to identify the sessions related to this job after the job starts and enable tracing from another session.

It was then necessary to obtain additional information like the name of the application server this job was running on, and the operating system user who was running the job. This information permitted narrowing the list of several hundred jobs running at that time to about a dozen. The *trace_other_12.sql* script was used to enable tracing for all of these target sessions. Tracing was stopped after a while though because one particular trace file had grown significantly larger than the rest.

At this point, another tool was considered to help analyze trace files. http://www.hotsos.com was contacted to request an evaluation copy of their Hotsos Profiler™ tool. The goal was to apply the tool for a quick and accurate solution to the performance problem. The trace file was analyzed, and then the output was reviewed. The analysis engine processed this very quickly. Figure 6.9 shows part of the first main screen of information.

```
Interval Resource Profile

Response Time Component                       Duration    # Calls
===================================  ===================  ==========
(i)  SQL*Net message from client     85.557003s   72.0%       59,345
(i)  CPU service                     15.020000s   12.6%      163,759
(i)  unaccounted-for                 13.167063s   11.1%
(i)  db file sequential read          4.877494s    4.1%        5,797
(i)  SQL*Net more data t client       0.067788s    0.1%        2,049
(i)  SQL*Net message to client        0.058038s    0.0%       59,345
(i)  latch free                       0.000742s    0.0%            1
===================================  ===================  ==========
Total                               118.748128s  100.0%
```

Figure 6.9 – *Hotsos Profiler: Interval Resource Profile*

The Interval Resource Profile is what Hotsos calls the breakdown, of the work done for the time that makes up this trace file interval. It provides a summary of the time that was spent working vs. waiting by this session during the time of this trace file. The Profile report also provides links to additional information as by the (i) before each event. This puts information about the specific events and what it means to the performance of this process a mouse-click away.

Other available information includes the impact various system components could possibly have on improving the performance of this process. In this case, any thoughts of upgrades to the storage system would not be practical since the only response-time component that would be impacted directly is *db file sequential read*, which only accounted for 4.1% of the response time for this trace file. Even though it would not be likely, if an upgrade to the storage system were to eliminate any file read waits, this would only reduce the time this job runs by only 4%, or less than 5 seconds for a 2-minute sample like this trace file.

In this trace file, the biggest Response Time Component is *SQL*Net message from client* which represents 72% of the time. The components will be underlined and hyperlinked on the Hotsos Profiler page. Clicking that link for this event brings up another section of the Profiler report as shown in Figure 6.10.

```
Contribution to Response Time Component by SQL Statement

(i) SQL*Net message from client

    SQL Statement ID                        Duration     #Calls
    ============================  ==================  =========
    3011837784                    11.149295s  13.0%      6,909
    3676874806                    11.100955s  13.0%      7,004
    1248877381                    10.750309s  12.6%      6,909
    3298763709                    10.600885s  12.4%      6,909
    148653422                     10.024905s  11.7%      6,909
    6 others                      31.930654s  37.3%     24,705
    ============================  ==================  =========
    Total                         85.557003s 100.0%     59,345
```

Figure 6.10 – *Hotsos Profiler: Response Time by SQL Statement*

The report in this figure shows the SQL statement ID, or hash value, for the top statements in terms of this Response Time Component. The first statement listed represents 13% of the time spent on this event. Since it is underlined and hyperlinked on the Hotsos Profiler page, click and view the information pertaining to this statement. Figure 6.11 displays the result.

```
Response Time Component                        Duration   # Calls
================================= ================== ==========
(i) SQL*Net message from client    11.149295s   75.9%      6,909
(i) CPU service                     2.220000s   15.1%     20,727
(i) db file sequential read         1.310613s    8.9%      1,199
(i) SQL*Net message to client       0.005918s    0.0%      6,909
================================= ================== ==========
Total                              14.685826s  100.0%
```

Figure 6.11 – *Hotsos Profiler: Statement Resource Profile*

This looks very similar to what was seen in Figure 6.9. The difference is this resource profile only represents the portion of the trace file that is related to a single SQL statement. Notice how the profile components are very similar between these two reports in terms of specific components as well as the ordering of the components. This seems to indicate that, even though the report in Figure 6.11 only shows the components for one SQL statement, what is affecting this statement may also be affecting all the statements listed in this trace file. Consequently, the information in Figure 6.11 does not provide any further understanding of the problem at hand. However, below the Statement Resource Profile, the report lists the Cumulative Database Call Statistics for this statement. See Figures 6.12 and 6.13. Figure 6.12 shows the leftmost columns of the report while Figure 6.13 shows the rightmost columns.

```
Statement Cumulative Database Call Statistics

Cursor  Library  Action      Rows  ------ Response Time ------
Action   Misses  Count  Processed  Elapsed       CPU     Other
-------  -------  -------  ---------  --------  --------  ---------
Parse          1    6,909          0  0.192655  0.210000  -0.017345
Execute        0    6,909          0  1.627567  1.710000  -0.082433
Fetch          0    6,909          6  1.543109  0.300000   1.243109
-------  -------  -------  ---------  --------  --------  ---------
Total          1   20,727          6  3.363331  2.220000   1.143331

Per Exe      0.0      1.0        0.0  0.000487  0.000321   0.000165
Per Row      0.2  1,151.5        1.0  0.560555  0.370000   0.190555
```

Figure 6.12 – *Hotsos Profiler: Database Call Statistics (part I)*

```
--------- LIO Blocks --------  ------- PIO Blocks --------
   Total  Consistent  Current    Total  Into SGA  Into PGA
--------  -----------  -------  --------  ---------  --------
       0            0        0         0          0         0
       0            0        0         0          0         0
  20,887       20,887        0     1,199      1,199         0
--------  -----------  -------  --------  ---------  --------
  20,887       20,887        0     1,199      1,199         0

     3.0          3.0      0.0       0.2        0.2       0.0
 3,481.2      3,481.2      0.0     199.8      199.8       0.0
```

Figure 6.13 – *Hotsos Profiler: Database Call Statistics (part II)*

Notice the breakdown of time spent on parsing and executing as well as the number of times these events happened for this statement. The total number of rows in the Fetch line is 6. On average, it took over 1,000 executions to get one row. One piece of information to make note of is the Action Count column which indicates that this statement was executed almost 7,000 times and was parsed the same number of times as it was executed. For some reason, it appears this statement is being parsed once for every time it executes which causes additional SQL*Net traffic. It is also responsible for unnecessary CPU utilization. Review Figure 6.9 and notice that CPU time is the number two component of this response time. Significantly reducing parse activity would reduce the two biggest components of this job. Reducing parsing activity to one parse to many executes is the goal. If this process were changed to eliminate all unnecessary parses, there is the very real potential of cutting the run time of this job by 50% or more.

If excessive parsing is a problem, the following script, *parse_v_execute.sql*, can be used for ongoing monitoring:

💾 *parse_v_execute.sql*

```
-- ************************************************
-- Copyright © 2003 by Rampant TechPress
-- This script is free for non-commercial purposes
-- with no warranties.  Use at your own risk.
--
-- To license this script for a commercial purpose,
-- contact info@rampant.cc
-- ************************************************

/* parse_v_execute.sql */
column sql_text          format a50
column parse_calls       format 9,999,999
column executions        format 9,999,999
column ratio             format 999.99     heading "Parse-
Execute|Ratio"
column loaded_versions format 999,999     heading "Loaded|Versions"
set pages 1000

select
   sql_text,
   parse_calls,
   executions,
   parse_calls/executions "Ratio",
   loaded_versions
from
   v$sql
where
   parsing_user_id !=0
and
   parse_calls     > 500
and
   executions      > 500
and
   rownum < 21
order by
   4 desc,
   3 desc;
```

To reduce the parsing, the following is recommended:

- Verify that the bind variables are application generated, not only database generated. Even database generated bind variables (via *cursor_sharing*=FORCE) require some parsing activity, and an application that uses bind variables instead of literal values will be more efficient and scalable.

  Use caution with this setting because Oracle RDBMS may still have some bugs related to *cursor_sharing*=FORCE. Adequate testing should be done before setting this parameter in production. See Metalink for more information.

- Review the application architecture and recommend compiler flags be tested to allow cursor sharing at the application level. For example, if the application is written in Pro*C, review the current usage of *hold_cursor* and *release_cursor* and understand the impact of the various combinations.

- Review the database cursor utilization with *cursor_usage.sql*. This script was discussed in a previous chapter and is available in the Code Depot.

Although it is possible that these recommendations could reduce the run-time of this job by 50% or more, in order to completely understand the 10046 trace and Profiler, the results of a deeper exploration will be covered.

Recall that in about 7,000 executions, this statement only returned six rows. Consequently, this means that most of those 7,000 executions were a waste of resources and completely unnecessary. The execution plan is displayed further down on the page below the Cumulative Database Call Statistics. The execution plan is very simple and shows that this statement is using an appropriate index.

The remaining solution seems to be to work with the development group to reduce the number of executions.

Although it is not an easy solution to implement, it is probably the best improvement that can be made. For example, if this job is a continuously running job that monitors for new data and processes any records that meet the condition, and if changing it to run once per minute will meet the business approval; then instead of running 3,500 times per minute, it will run one time per minute. This will reduce the load on the server and allow the current server to meet the required load for a lot longer. If this job can be changed to handle multiple rows at a time instead of single row at a time, the amount of wasted resources on this system will drop considerably.

Conclusion

This chapter has demonstrated the use of event 10046 to obtain extended SQL trace information. It also demonstrated three of the ways available to analyze that data; manual analysis, Trace Analyzer from Oracle, and Hotsos Profiler from hotsos.com. Different situations may call for different tools and several options have been shown here for troubleshooting performance problems.

The next chapter will cover various ways the STATSPACK utility can be used to gather system-wide information that will be useful for troubleshooting performance problems.

Using STATSPACK

Introduction

In a previous chapter, various ways to use STATSPACK were presented. It was explained that STATSPACK could be used for reactive tuning as well as proactive tuning. Proactive tuning is always preferred since the idea is to prevent problems before they are noticed by users. However, unless the DBA has the ability to see into the future, it is unlikely that there will be an accurate prediction of the future. Therefore, in this chapter, STATSPACK will be presented an effective tool to troubleshoot performance in a reactive mode.

The use of Event 10046 to obtain extended SQL tracing data involves an evaluation of performance from a user-level and the correction of problems that are affecting specific users. When the problem is well-defined to the degree that specific users can be identified, the use of this approach is effective and highly recommended by experienced DBAs.

There are many times, when for a variety of technical and/or organizational reasons, information on the specific session or user that is performing poorly is not available. Frequently, the mechanism by which performance problems come to light is that management of a client company simply states that customers are complaining about performance, so they turn to the DBA to resolve the problem. At these times, the DBA must examine performance starting at a higher level, and then dig down until the level of detail that can either provide them with a solution or point them to a specific session is achieved. Therefore, the lessons learned about extended SQL tracing can be applied.

Don't let user complaints about system performance make you crazy.

Setting-Up STATSPACK

If STATSPACK is used to tune a performance problem, the first step is the installation of the product. STATSPACK is shipped with most versions of Oracle. If a user's version of Oracle is one of the few that does not have STATSPACK, then a copy can be obtained from Oracle.

There is no point in duplicating documentation that Oracle already provides, so this section will not attempt to repeat the information available on Metalink in documents like Note 149113.1. This Note provides instructions for installing and configuring STATSPACK. This chapter will only highlight the basic process and mention a few important things to keep in mind when installing STATSPACK.

The install process is initiated by running the *spcreate.sql* script while connected to SQL*Plus as *sysdba*. *Spcreate.sql* is short for STATSPACK create. The STATSPACK scripts are prefixed with "sp" which makes them easier to remember. The default location for the creation script, as well as the additional STATSPACK scripts, is the *rdbms/admin* subdirectory of the Oracle Home.

Before running this script, it is helpful to make a list of the tablespaces that are available for storing the STATSPACK repository data. For many reasons, the STATSPACK repository should not be installed into the *system* tablespace. The installation script is designed to abort if this is attempted. When prompted for a tablespace name, choose a tablespace designated for tools. The installation script will list the available tablespaces before prompting for a choice. If there are only a few tablespaces, using the prompt will work; however, if there are many tablespaces, it may be easier to query for a list of tablespaces with the name *tool* as part of the name if that is the naming standard.

Also, if an older version of Oracle that includes the *svrmgrl* program is being used, DO NOT use this program to install STATSPACK. *svrmgrl* does not support some of the commands that are part of the install script. In this instance, SQL*Plus should be used instead of *svrmgrl*.

The install should be fairly simple and painless. It will create the tables and packages that will be used for monitoring database statistics. It will also create a user called PERFSTAT with a default password of PERFSTAT. Oracle Note 160861.1 contains a recommendation for changing the default password for security reasons.

Gathering Statistics

After installing STATSPACK, the next step is to begin gathering data that can then be analyzed and compiled into information related to a performance problem. Gathering data with STATSPACK involves an activity called 'taking a snapshot.' For those users that work with Oracle replication, it is important to understand that a STATSPACK snapshot has absolutely nothing to do with snapshots in replication. A STATSPACK snapshot is more along the lines of a snapshot that would be taken while on vacation, otherwise known as a photograph. This kind of snapshot represents information that was in the system views and tables at the time when the snapshot was taken.

If STATSPACK has already been installed, it is easy to take a snapshot to get started. Simply login to the database as the PERFSTAT user and run the command to execute the snapshot procedure. This procedure is called *snap* and is in the *statspack* package.

```
execute statspack.snap;
```

This command, when executed from the SQL*Plus prompt, results in data being collected from the system views and tables. That data is stored in the STATSPACK repository created earlier. This command is simple and the typical output looks like Figure 7.1.

```
SQL> execute statspack.snap;

PL/SQL procedure successfully completed.
```

Figure 7.1 – *Results of taking a STATSPACK snapshot*

Frequency

After taking the initial snapshot, allow a short period time to pass and then repeat the process. As soon as there are at least two snapshots with no database downtime in between, prepare a report on the database activity during that interval. The length of the time interval is the subject of a great deal of debate among DBAs. Ideally, the interval should be just long enough so that the problem-related statistics will be completely collected, but short enough to omit other statistics which might obscure the relevant data. The goal is to avoid a condition in which the spike in the statistics that indicate the problem gets 'averaged-out' of the picture.

If STATSPACK is run via a cron job or from a job scheduling package, it can easily be scheduled to run at a frequency ranging from once every minute to once a month or anywhere in between. The trick is to find the balance between too often and not often enough. For most reactive tuning situations, snapshots taken at intervals from five to fifteen minutes apart will provide a reasonable amount of data to make a good start on tuning.

An important thing to remember is that even if statistics are gathered too frequently with STATSPACK, reporting can always be done on a larger time window. For example, if snapshots are at five-minute intervals and there is a report that takes 30 minutes to run, that report may or may not be slow during any given five-minute period. After looking at the five-minute windows, the DBA can decide to look at a 30-minute window and then run a report that spans six individual five-minute windows. The moral of the story is to err on the side of sampling too often rather than not often enough.

History

Once the frequency for of the snapshots has been determined, the DBA will need to decide how long to retain the data from those snapshots.

Data will need to be gathered over a long enough period of time to isolate significant trends. The end-points of the STATSPACK report will ideally encompass a statistically relevant period of business activity. For example, a one-week trend of increasing statistics is not enough if the business is one, like the mortgage business, which is slow at the beginning of the month, builds throughout the month and ends with peak activity around the last day of the month. In this case, an early, mid, and late month baseline load against which to compare a given report will need to be collected. If a typical system load profile is available, the DBA can use that information to get a better understanding of the business cycle. Until complete business cycle information is available, keep the collected data longer.

Make sure to gather data over an adequate time period.

It is important to remember that there will be no data to use for tuning if tablespace room is exhausted and the snapshots start failing. Filling up a tablespace with STATSPACK data could cause other processes that require room in the same tablespace to fail. This is another good reason to put STATSPACK data in a dedicated tablespace, or at least in a tablespace that is not shared with business applications. While it is not good for tuning purposes to have monitoring tools fail, such tool failures are preferable to having a business application fail due to the retention of too much STATSPACK data.

Once the appropriate amount of historical STATSPACK data for the situation has been determined, implement a process to periodically purge the STATSPACK data. This task became easier in Oracle9i because the *spurge.sql* script was added and some omissions in integrity constraints were corrected. The *spurge.sql* script can be used interactively, or it can be called in batch mode. Using *spurge.sql* in batch mode is useful for automated maintenance since a query can be written to pass script values to purge all data older than *n* days. It is recommended that the "pruning" of STATSPACK snapshots be accomplished via a regularly scheduled job. In fact, "housecleaning" could even be added to the STATSPACK snapshot job so that outdated snapshots are automatically removed before new snapshots are taken. This is a "best practice" since the problems and risks that could arise by depending on running the purge manually can be avoided. Several useful scripts are available in Don Burleson's book, "*High Performance Tuning with STATSPACK*", which is recommended as a resource for maximizing the potential of STATSPACK.

Using *spreport.sql*

spreport.sql is the script that Oracle supplies with STATSPACK to create a report based upon STATSPACK snapshot data. When used interactively, it prompts the user for the "start" and "stop" snapshot ids and then prepares a report showing the difference in the values for many of the *v$* views that are part of the Wait Interface.

By using *spreport.sql*, it is possible to quickly learn what is going on in the database. The following figures contain a few sections of the report:

```
STATSPACK report for

DB Name          DB Id Instance Inst Num  Release Cluster Host
---------- ---------- -------- -------- --------- ------- -------
TOY        2410677970 TOY            1 9.2.0.3.0 NO      matthew

             Snap Id       Snap Time    Sessions Curs/Sess Comment
             ------- ------------------ -------- --------- ----------
Begin Snap:      821 10-Jan-04 23:26:37        8       5.1
  End Snap:      823 12-Jan-04 22:44:10        8       5.1
   Elapsed:              2,837.55 (mins)

Cache Sizes (end)
~~~~~~~~~~~~~~~~~
            Buffer Cache:       12M    Std Block Size:       16K
        Shared Pool Size:        8M        Log Buffer:       32K
```

Figure 7.2 – *STATSPACK Report Header Information*

Figure 7.2 shows the first part of the report produced by *spreport.sql*. This section contains the database name and id number, the instance name and version information, and the start and finish time for the report. The sizes of the various caches at the time the "stop" snapshot was taken are shown at the bottom of Figure 7.2.

```
Load Profile
~~~~~~~~~~~~                        Per Second    Per Transaction
                                    ----------    ---------------
               Redo size:              10.80          367,622.40
           Logical reads:               1.77           60,138.00
           Block changes:               0.05            1,667.60
          Physical reads:               0.13            4,347.00
         Physical writes:               0.01              195.40
              User calls:               0.01              361.80
                  Parses:               0.02              665.20
             Hard parses:               0.00               28.40
                   Sorts:               0.20            6,818.20
                  Logons:               0.00                0.60
                Executes:               0.42           14,162.60
            Transactions:               0.00
% Blocks changed per Read:    2.77       Recursive Call %: 99.14
Rollback per transaction %:   0.00       Rows per Sort:    0.57
```

Figure 7.3 – *SPREPORT Load Profile*

Earlier, while learning about the Hotsos Profiler, there was a section with a resource profile. That resource profile was used to show the various response-time components. Similarly, the Load Profile section in the STATSPACK report is a characterization of the amount of work that the database was doing during the report interval. The components are measured in two ways; per second and per transaction. These components are statistics just like logical and physical reads as well as parsing, sorting and other methods used to measure how busy a database is.

Each of the elements in the Load Profile contributes to the amount of time it takes to process any given statement. For example, if users are reporting widespread problems with performance, and the number of sorts per second is significantly higher than it was during the baseline measurement, it may be helpful to look for any recently introduced code with heavy sort activity. This could be related to code that is performing unnecessary sorts or to an increase in the normal amount of data being sorted, and may require an adjustment in the *sort_area_size* for some or all users.

If there is a baseline measurement available, the Load Profile section of this report is a good place to start the analysis. If the baseline is from a time when there was user consensus that performance was good, then the Load Profile from a "bad" period can be compared to the baseline to help find any discrepancies.

```
Instance Efficiency Percentages (Target 100%)
~~~~~~~~~~~~~~~~~~~~~~~~~~~~~~~~~~~~~~~~~~~~~~~~~
            Buffer Nowait %:   100.00    Redo NoWait %:   100.00
            Buffer Hit    %:    92.80  In-memory Sort %:    99.98
            Library Hit   %:    98.97      Soft Parse %:    95.73
         Execute to Parse %:    95.30       Latch Hit %:   100.00
Parse CPU to Parse Elapsed %:    41.47    % Non-Parse CPU:    73.16

Shared Pool Statistics         Begin      End
                              -------    ------
            Memory Usage %:     95.70     95.68
   % SQL with executions>1:     69.23     85.19
   % Memory for SQL w/exec>1:   46.21     56.05
```

Figure 7.4 – *SPREPORT Efficiency Percentages*

The percentages shown in Figure 7.4 are, in fact, the often maligned ratios. There has been much debate in the DBA community about ratios as a tool for measuring performance, but the ratios are included in the SPREPORT, so it is important that DBAs understand when and how to use them in ways to benefit themselves and other users.

The "Buffer Hit" and "Buffer Nowait" numbers are only valid for comparison and trend analysis for the same instance and across a sufficient time interval. A single SQL statement with a large number of logical or physical reads could severely influence these values and not have a significant impact on any given user's operations. A "good" ratio in one database may be a "terrible" ratio in another, so it is not advisable to compare these numbers across different databases. A Buffer Cache Hit Ratio (BCHR) is only valid when comparing snapshots from two different periods of time for a given database.

The "Execute to Parse" ratio is an important metric. If the database server is parsing every statement that is executing, this ratio will be close to 1% while the best case scenario is 100% which would indicate an application that "parses once and executes many times".

If users are complaining about application performance, the system capacity is stretched, or maybe there are concerns about the scalability of the database, the "Execute to Parse" ratio can be one valid indicator of a problem. If the ratio is too low, it is possible that the application is not using shareable SQL, or the database has sub-optimal parameters that are reducing the effectiveness of cursor sharing. A problem like excessive parsing is likely to manifest itself as additional network traffic between the application server and clients. The additional parse activity may also show up as a marked increase in CPU consumption on the database server.

When excessive parsing is part of a performance problem, hard parsing is usually the biggest contributor. Soft parsing is less of a performance issue, but it can still negatively impact database performance in a significant way. In applications where there are connections to the database that are opened and closed frequently and repeatedly, cursor sharing can suffer. Opening and closing database connections also carries some additional overhead.

In cases where this is an issue, regular monitoring of parsing is important. In addition, when the "Execute to Parse" ratio is lower than the baseline for a given instance, find out what specific SQL statements have a parse count that is equal to the execute count. These statements are contributing to ineffective cursor sharing. In either of these situations, the following script is useful because it calculates a related ratio using SQL statement.

parse_v_execute.sql results are interpreted the opposite from the STATSPACK ratio, in that a higher a score or ratio indicates a lower effectiveness of that particular statement in terms of the goal of "parse once – execute many".

🖫 parse_v_execute.sql

```
-- ****************************************************
-- Copyright © 2003 by Rampant TechPress
-- This script is free for non-commercial purposes
-- with no warranties.  Use at your own risk.
--
-- To license this script for a commercial purpose,
-- contact info@rampant.cc
-- ****************************************************

column sql_text            format a50
column parse_calls         format 9,999,999
column executions          format 9,999,999
column ratio               format 999.99     heading "Parse-
Execute|Ratio"
column loaded_versions format 999,999     heading "Loaded|Versions"
set pages 1000

select
   sql_text,
   parse_calls,
   executions,
   parse_calls/executions "Ratio"
from
   v$sql
where
   parsing_user_id !=0
and
   parse_calls       > 500
and
   executions        > 500
and
   rownum < 21
order by
   4 desc,
   3 desc;
```

```
                                                      Parse-Execute    Loaded
SQL-TEXT                              PARSE_CALLS EXECUTIONS    Ratio  Versions
------------------------------------- ----------- ---------- ------------- --------
BEGIN DBMS_APPLICATION_INFO.SET_MODULE(:1,NUL      15        15      1.00        1
L); END;

BEGIN DBMS_OUTPUT.DISABLE; END;                    15        15      1.00        1
SELECT USER FROM DUAL                              15        15      1.00        1
SELECT NULL FROM DUAL FOR UPDATE NOWAIT            15        15      1.00        1
SELECT DECODE('A','A','1','2') FROM DUAL           15        15      1.00        1
SELECT ATTRIBUTE,SCOPE,NUMERIC_VALUE,CHAR_VAL      13        13      1.00        1
UE,DATE_VALUE FROM SYSTEM.PRODUCT_PRIVS WHERE
(UPPER('SQL*Plus') LIKE UPPER(PRODUCT)) AND (
UPPER(USER) LIKE USERID)
```

Figure 7.5 – *Parse to Execute SQL Effectiveness Analysis*

To correctly understand Figure 7.5, remember that it was generated by a top-n style query. After eliminating some "uninteresting" rows with low executions and parses, the top 20 rows in the report are the worst offenders in terms of failure to meet our "parse once – execute many" goal. Unless a report starts with scores closer to 0 than 1, making changes to allow any of these items to make better use of cursors should have a major positive impact on the performance and scalability of the application. By including the *loaded_versions* as well, the low numbers indicate that these SQL statements are not being shared.

Using oraperf.com

Anjo Kolk, an Oracle scientist who was one of the early users of the Wait Interface, determined that in order to properly tune an Oracle database, it made little sense to reduce contention or improve performance any component that only represented a small percentage of the total time spent. He co-authored a paper in 1999 titled, "Yet Another Performance Profiling Method (Or YAPP-Method)", which explained the reasoning behind this philosophy. This paper launched Wait Interface methodology outside the walls of Oracle Corporation.

Anjo created OraPerf.com, a web page where STATSPACK reports can be uploaded. Predecessor reports such as

UTLBSTAT and UTLESTAT are also available. After users generate a report with the *spreport.sql* and upload it to OraPerf.com, the web page quickly generates an analysis. This analysis allows for a quick evaluation of possible causes of a performance problem. Following the Yet Another Performance Profiling (YAPP) method, Figure 7.6 shows the breakdown of the response time into broad categories that represent the status of events that were working or waiting.

	Time	Percentage	Response Time Per Execute	Per User Call	Per Transaction
Response Time	15750	100.00%	0.22	199.37	0.00
CPU Time	12650	80.32%	0.17	160.13	0.00
Wait Time	3100	19.68%	0.04	39.24	0.00

Figure 7.6 – *OraPerf.com Response Time Breakdown*

Figure 7.6 illustrates that regardless of the stated goal of tuning based on wait events, it is impossible to ignore that working time, indicated by CPU Time, is likely a better target for tuning. OraPerf.com provides a CPU Time hyperlink that opens another part of the report that shows a further breakdown of that category. That part of the report is shown in Figure 7.7.

		CPU Time			
	Time	Percentage	Per Execute	Per User Call	Per Transaction
Total	12650	100.00%	0.17	160.13	0.00
Parse CPU Time	208	1.64%	0.00	2.63	0.00
Recursive CPU Time	11915	94.19%	0.16	150.82	0.00
Other CPU Time	527	4.17%	0.01	6.67	0.00

Figure 7.7 – *OraPerf.com CPU Time Breakdown*

Since Recursive CPU Time accounts for over 94% of the CPU time, it is clear that tuning this database will require either an overall a reduction of this work category or an increase in its efficiency.

Using Manual Script Analysis

Another way to use STATSPACK is to run scripts against the STATSPACK data repository to look for statistical trends. Negative trends can be corrected before system performance suffers enough that users begin to notice a problem.

This section is intended to demonstrate a few ways to use STATSPACK to tune a database. See the Reference section at the end of the book for additional resources on maximizing the use of STATSPACK.

One example of trend analysis available from STATSPACK data is the report produced by the following script: *sp_bhr_trend.sql*. This report shows the buffer hit ratio for each of the buffer pools: *DEFAULT; KEEP;* and *RECYCLE*. If these pools have been implemented, it makes sense to monitor the buffer hit ratio. The goal is to have a high *KEEP* ratio, a low *RECYCLE* ratio, and a *DEFAULT* ratio that falls somewhere in between. Maintaining a high ratio for the *KEEP* pool, however, should not be the driving force for tuning. It is unlikely that an increase in the *KEEP* pool ratio alone will resolve user performance problems.

🖫 sp_bhr_trend.sql

```
-- *************************************************
-- Copyright © 2003 by Rampant TechPress
-- This script is free for non-commercial purposes
-- with no warranties.  Use at your own risk.
--
-- To license this script for a commercial purpose,
-- contact info@rampant.cc
-- *************************************************

/* sp_bhr_trend.sql */
column bhr format 9.99
column mydate heading 'Year Mo Dy Ht'
select
   to_char(snap_time,'yyyy-mm-dd HH24')      mydate,
   new.name                                  buffer_pool_name,
   (((new.consistent_gets - old.consistent_gets) +
   (new.db_block_gets - old.db_block_gets)) -
   (new.physical_reads - old.physical_reads))
   /
   ((new.consistent_gets - old.consistent_gets) +
   (new.db_block_gets - old.db_block_gets))   bhr
from
   perfstat.stats$buffer_pool_statistics old,
   perfstat.stats$buffer_pool_statistics new,
   perfstat.stats$snapshot                    sn
where
   new.name = old.name
and
   new.snap_id = sn.snap_id
and
   old.snap_id = sn.snap_id - 1
and
   sn.snap_time >= (sysdate -7)
order by
   1 asc;
```

sp_bhr_trend.sql provides insight into the appropriateness of the sizes of the various buffer pools. By default, it allows a view of the hourly ratio for each of the pools, assuming that STATSPACK is set to take snapshots at least one time per hour. This is a good starting point, and an analysis of a one-day sample or multiple-day results will yield a more complete assessment of the system. Figure 7.8 shows the output of this query for a given database that appears to only have one snapshot per day.

```
Year Mo Dy Hr BUFFER_POOL_NAME   BHR
------------- ---------------- -----
2004-01-10 00 KEEP               .93
2004-01-10 00 RECYCLE            .96
2004-01-10 00 DEFAULT            .99
2004-01-11 00 KEEP               .82
2004-01-11 00 RECYCLE            .88
2004-01-11 00 DEFAULT            .99
2004-01-12 00 KEEP               .80
2004-01-12 00 RECYCLE            .96
2004-01-12 00 DEFAULT            .99
2004-01-13 00 KEEP               .94
2004-01-13 00 RECYCLE            .96
2004-01-13 00 DEFAULT            .99
2004-01-14 00 KEEP               .94
2004-01-14 00 RECYCLE            .96
2004-01-14 00 DEFAULT            .99
2004-01-16 00 KEEP               .93
2004-01-16 00 RECYCLE            .59
2004-01-16 00 DEFAULT            .99
```

Figure 7.8 – *Using STATSPACK data for trend analysis of buffer cache ratios*

This data could be easily imported into a spreadsheet and used to make graphs and charts for clearer analysis. In addition, there are a number of utilities that provide a graphical front-end for the STATSPACK data.

Another script, *sp_sorts_ratio_trend.sql*, shows the percentage of sorts that take place in memory compared to on disk. When too many sorts happen on disk, a bottleneck can be introduced. This can cause additional disk I/O. This additional I/O could result in run speed reduction for both the sorting session as well as any other session that has to wait longer for disk access.

🖫 sp_sorts_ratio_trend.sql

```
-- ***************************************************
-- Copyright © 2003 by Rampant TechPress
-- This script is free for non-commercial purposes
-- with no warranties.  Use at your own risk.
--
-- To license this script for a commercial purpose,
-- contact info@rampant.cc
-- ***************************************************

/* sp_sorts_ratio_trend.sql */
column SNAP_DATE heading "Year Mo Day Hour" format a16
column MEMORY_SORTS                          format 999,999,999
column DISK_SORTS                            format 999,999,999
column "DISK/MEMORY RATIO"                   format 999.99
select
   to_char(snap_time, 'yyyy-mm-dd HH24') SNAP_DATE,
   memnew.value-memold.value MEMORY_SORTS,
   disknew.value-diskold.value DISK_SORTS,
   (((disknew.value-diskold.value) /
   (memnew.value-memold.value)) * 100)
   "DISK/MEMORY RATIO"
from
   perfstat.stats$sysstat MEMOLD,
   perfstat.stats$sysstat MEMNEW,
   perfstat.stats$sysstat DISKNEW,
   perfstat.stats$sysstat DISKOLD,
   perfstat.stats$snapshot sp
where
   disknew.snap_id = sp.snap_id
and
   diskold.snap_id = sp.snap_id-1
and
   memnew.snap_id = sp.snap_id
and
   memold.snap_id = sp.snap_id-1
and
   memold.name = 'sorts (memory)'
and
   memnew.name = 'sorts (memory)'
and
   diskold.name = 'sorts (disk)'
and
   disknew.name = 'sorts (disk)'
and
   memnew.value - memold.value > 0
and
   disknew.value - diskold.value > 0
and
   trunc(sp.snap_time) > '&Start_Time_dd_mon_yy'
order by
   snap_date
;
```

This script takes a slightly different approach to the date range used for reporting. The script prompts the user for the start date and only displays data from snapshots that were taken after that date. It would be easy to modify this script by adding a parameter to schedule a weekly job to run this query with a start time of one week ago. The output from that type of a job could be used for ongoing monitoring in order to detect or troubleshoot a performance problem. For example, Figure 7.9 shows an execution of this script. This sample yields no ratio that would be worth worrying about. However, if the users had complained that that on Friday January 9th performance was terrible, the DBA would want to dig deeper and find out why the number of sorts increased by almost around 700% compared to other Fridays.

```
Enter value for start_time_dd_mon_yy: 01-jan-2004

Year Mo Day Hour MEMORY_SORTS  DISK_SORTS  DISK/MEMORY RATIO
---------------- ------------  ----------  -----------------
2004-01-02  00       264,432       44                   .02
2004-01-03  00       249,125       34                   .01
2004-01-04  00       240,011       30                   .01
2004-01-05  00       231,886       27                   .01
2004-01-06  00       778,836       45                   .01
2004-01-07  00       338,359       41                   .01
2004-01-08  00       273,514       48                   .02
2004-01-09  00     1,646,303       43                   .00
2004-01-10  00       225,689       36                   .02
2004-01-11  00       229,188       41                   .02
2004-01-12  00       210,382       32                   .02
2004-01-13  00       414,357       48                   .01
2004-01-14  00       264,278       43                   .02
2004-01-15  00       251,745       42                   .02
2004-01-16  00       257,429       41                   .02
```

Figure 7.9 – *Using STATSPACK data for trend analysis of sort activity*

Extending STATSPACK

There are areas where STATSPACK does not ordinarily capture data. Statistics like free memory and CPU utilization are two data points that can be important indicators of a problem. Using tools like *vmstat*, a DBA can look at these statistics, but it is not possible to go back to a point in time and see what was going on. There are ways to extend STATSPACK so that when a snapshot is taken, it will gather information from the operating system and store it in another table.

Gathering additional information in this way is a great way to enhance the STATSPACK tool and overcome some its weaknesses. More information on how to do this can be found in the resources listed in the References at the end of this book.

Step-by-Step Examples and Case Studies

Case #1 – Buffer Cache Tuning

The first case deals with a typical problem. A trouble ticket has been opened and assigned to the DBA. The complaint is that the application is running slowly. Therefore, the DBA is asked to "make the database faster". This is not a foreign request to a DBA.

STATSPACK was previously installed, and the DBA is unable to immediately determine that any specific userid is being affected more than others; therefore, the DBA will take a few snapshots and gather about a two-minute interval of data.

After getting the snapshots, the DBA runs *spreport.sql* and looks at the report. Figure 7.10 shows the first section to be viewed.

```
Instance Efficiency Percentages (Target 100%)
~~~~~~~~~~~~~~~~~~~~~~~~~~~~~~~~~~~~~~~~~~~~~~~~
            Buffer Nowait %:   100.00    Redo NoWait %:   100.00
              Buffer Hit   %:    30.48    In-memory Sort %:   99.27
             Library Hit   %:    89.09       Soft Parse %:    92.36
          Execute to Parse %:    28.67       Latch Hit %:    100.00
   Parse CPU to Parse Elapsed%:    81.37    % Non-Parse CPU:    89.55
```

Figure 7.10 – *SPREPORT with low buffer hit ratio*

The Buffer Hit Percentage is only 30.48%. In light of the focus on Wait Event tuning, the importance of the Buffer Cache Hit Ratio was downplayed earlier. While there is validity to the arguments against hit-ratio tuning, there are times when this process might prove useful. In particular, this low ratio which is for the whole buffer pool may cause the DBA to investigate further to see if performance can be gained via the buffer cache.

v$buffer_pool_statistics presents information on how the various pools are being used. Calculate the ratio for each configured pool and note, in figure 7.11, that the *KEEP* and *RECYCLE* pool are not being used. Then dig in to find out which object is requested the most and evaluate it for assignment to the *KEEP* pool.

```
NAME                            HIT_RATIO
------------------------------  ---------
DEFAULT                             54.71
```

Figure 7.11 – *Single Buffer Cache with Low Hit Ratio*

Looking further down in the STATSPACK report, there is a way to determine which SQL statement had the biggest impact on the buffer cache hit ratio. The STATSPACK report contains a section that shows the SQL statements ordered by database gets. See Figure 7.12 to see this part of the report.

```
                                                  CPU      Elapsed
Buffer Gets Executions Gets per Exec %Total Time (s)  Time (s) Hash Value
----------- ---------- ------------- ------ -------- -------- ----------
      7,646          6       1,274.3   44.4     5.94     7.85 4265037669
Module: sqlplus@matthew (TNS V1-V3)
Select * from foo
```

Figure 7.12 – *SQL Statements by Database Gets*

The SQL statement is a select from the table named "foo", so it is desirable to get more information about "foo". In this case, the script *segment_info.sql* can be used to find out more about a segment which is a table.

🖫 segment_info.sql

```
-- ****************************************************
-- Copyright © 2003 by Rampant TechPress
-- This script is free for non-commercial purposes
-- with no warranties.  Use at your own risk.
--
-- To license this script for a commercial purpose,
-- contact info@rampant.cc
-- ****************************************************
select
   segment_name,
   partition_name,
   segment_type,
   tablespace_name,
   sum(bytes)/1024/1024 "MBytes"
from
   dba_extents
where
   segment_name = upper('&Segment_Name')
and
   owner = upper ('&Owner')
group by
   segment_name,
   partition_name,
   segment_type,
   tablespace_name;
```

```
SEGMENT_NAME    PART_   SEGMENT_TYPE    TABLESPACE_NAME   Mbytes
-------------   ------  -------------   ----------------  -------
FOO                     TABLE           USERS              1.00
```

Figure 7.13 – *Segment Information for an object*

Notice that this table is about 1 MB in size. Theorize that a *KEEP* pool of at least 1 MB in size is created, and mark this table to be kept in that pool, the physical I/Os should drop and performance should improve. The fact that the hit ratio for the *KEEP* pool would be high is of no importance to the user, so it is regarded as a collateral benefit to keep monitoring tools happy.

Reconfigure the database so that it has a *KEEP* pool of 2 MB. This will require a database restart unless the application is at least version 9. Configure table "foo" to put it into the *KEEP* pool that was just created. The following command will accomplish this goal:

```
alter table foo storage (buffer_pool KEEP);
```

In order to examine the results, query the user and run another STATSPACK report for a similar period of time to look for the code seen earlier while accessing this table. Reviewing the new report, it is evident that while this SQL statement is still there, it no longer impacts the user as much since it can almost always get the data from the buffer cache. As a side benefit, notice that the Buffer Hit ratio is significantly higher now as shown in Figure 7.14. This does not necessarily mean that the performance is better, but it is back to what is considered "normal" for this database.

```
Instance Efficiency Percentages (Target 100%)
~~~~~~~~~~~~~~~~~~~~~~~~~~~~~~~~~~~~~~~~~~~~~~~~~~
            Buffer Nowait %:    100.00      Redo NoWait %:    100.00
            Buffer Hit   %:      99.58   In-memory Sort %:     98.64
            Library Hit  %:     100.00      Soft Parse %:     100.00
          Execute to Parse %:    37.68       Latch Hit %:     100.00
 Parse CPU to Parse Elapsed%:   119.05    % Non-Parse CPU:     98.32
```

Figure 7.14 – *SPREPORT with higher buffer hit ratio*

Another area to consider is whether the SQL statement in question is really needed. If this SQL statement is a scheduled job that runs on a regular basis, it may be possible that there is no longer a business need to continue running this job. For example, a daily report could have been rendered obsolete by a new screen that provides up-to-the-minute data.

If the SQL statement does pass that test, then another question to ask is whether or not it can be optimized. Optimizing could reduce the load on the database and make overall performance better.

Case #2 – I/O Tuning

This case demonstrates that sometimes it does not matter, as much, what the sampling frequency is, but that sampling is done regularly. Trend analysis can be an immensely valuable tool when dealing with intermittent performance issues.

For example, assume that the performance of a daily batch job has been an issue from time to time. The job runs daily and is scheduled to finish before the majority of the users arrive in the morning; however, it was sometimes still running when users arrived and it adversely impacted user performance. This problem was difficult to troubleshoot because it did not happen every day, but seemed to crop up once or twice a month. By using STATSPACK data, the problem became apparent after looking at trend data over a period of time.

At the time that the users reported this problem, the analysis of wait events indicated a high level of file-related waits. It usually takes a period of time for a problem to be reported by the users. By the time information about this particular problem reached the DBA, it was too late. There was no "smoking gun" session that was consuming an inordinate amount of I/O. The users then reported improving performance until things were back to normal.

After several iterations of responding to this problem in a reactive manner, the DBA took a step back and looked at the history of when this problem was occurring. All of the reported incidents took place on either the first business day or the sixteenth day of the month. Any time the 1st or 16th calendar day landed on a working day, there were problems.

Since STATSPACK had been running for some time in this database, trend analysis on I/O levels was performed using existing reports that had been generated with SPREPORT. Figure 7.15 shows the data that stands out under a simple analysis of the file.

A quick note about trend reports is probably in order at this point. When many DBAs think of trend analysis, they think of running SQL commands against a database-based repository of information much like STATSPACK. This example shows how the STATSPACK reports, which are simple text files, can be used to examine a trend over time. To effectively do this, regular STATSPACK reports should be run and named in a standard manner. In most cases, the default names should work. A purge process setup would help to avoid the need for manually handling housekeeping chores. It also makes sense to have the new report generated at the same time as the oldest report is cleaned up if it is more than *n* days old.

```
oracle:/work$ cat sp*1ˢᵗ | grep Logical
            Logical reads:              149.70            5,738.33
            Logical reads:                5.56            6,286.00
            Logical reads:               67.22                7.50
            Logical reads:               67.75                6.82
            Logical reads:               68.85                6.74
            Logical reads:               85.21                8.70
            Logical reads:              349.98           22,398.50
```

Figure 7.15 – *SPREPORT data in a trend analysis*

Among other things, looking at the number of logical reads per second for some of these reports shows that from a normal of 70-80 it jumps to 150-350 in a few cases. Further research indicated that the spikes happened on the days when the batch process ran late.

Now, progress is being made. The window of the problem was narrowed and it was identified that the batch process was running late due to the additional I/O on these days. Conducting a more detailed analysis on specific STATSPACK reports revealed the exact SQL statements responsible for the large spike in logical reads. The culprit process was an extraction from the database, subsequently used for a data warehouse load, which took place on the 1st and 16th day of the month. Since the extract job was scheduled regardless of whether or not the day occurred on a weekend, this conflict was not predictable enough to correlate the two events.

Having identified the problem, tuning was then undertaken on the data warehouse extract process to make it more efficient. This allowed the extract to take place without adversely impacting the batch process that had been impacting the users.

Conclusion

In this chapter, the advantages of working with STATSPACK to gather data about the database performance were presented. It is clear that STATSPACK will allow for both proactive and reactive activities. The benefits of using an analysis tool were explained and demonstrated. Ways to analyze trends using the standard output from *spreport.sql* were shown.

Some of the ways to use STATSPACK go beyond the scope of this book on Wait Event tuning, such as extending STATSPACK to gather information about the operating system statistics and performance. More help on that is available in the texts listed in the reference section of this book.

The next section of this book will introduce some of the new Wait Event features in 10g. Most of what has been covered so far will work with either little or no modifications, but there are new options in 10g that may benefit tuning activities.

Overview of 10g

Introduction

In previous chapters, ways to use Wait Interface to enhance performance have been discussed. The topics covered so far apply to the various versions of Oracle released since the Wait Interface was introduced in version 7. The continual improvements in the information tracked by the Wait Interface have made it more effective over time. With the introduction of version 10g, the information tracked by the Wait Interface has again increased in quantity, value, and utility. In addition, there are other new performance enhancements.

Features like Active Session History (ASH), Automatic Database Diagnostic Monitor (ADDM), and enhancements to Enterprise Manager increase the effectiveness of Oracle database tuning when using the Wait Interface. Other improvements make some of the queries previously printed somewhat simpler. Joining *v$session* to *v$session_wait* is no longer required in Oracle10g since some of the key information in *v$session_wait* is now included in *v$session* and its related structures.

This chapter will introduce the enhancements available in release 1 of Oracle 10g. Later chapters will cover areas where Oracle 10g has dramatically improved in the area of database tuning, and will present examples of how to effectively apply the Wait Interface tuning methodology.

Licensing

Some of the new features that will be discussing are separately licensed products. Each separately licensed component will not be discussed in detail; however, general information about the components available at the time of this writing will be included. It is up to each Oracle customer considering an upgrade to 10g to review the feature set included in any given version (Enterprise, Standard, Standard One and Personal), and decide which feature set makes the most business sense for them. If a separately licensed feature is appealing and could sway the decision on which version will be purchased, this should be discussed early and often in negotiations with the sales representative.

"No, an Oracle license is not a valid substitute for a driver's license."

Without trying to explain the intricate details of Oracle's licensing, the essence is that Oracle requires special licensing to access the AWR (Automatic Workload Repository) and ADDM features. These licensing requirements cover simple SQL queries of certain data dictionary objects, procedures, and packages. This is in addition to the graphical front-end that is part of the Enterprise Manager.

Many of these features support Oracle's assertion that 10g is easier to manage than previous versions. Obviously, the new features have required many man-hours to develop and test, so it is reasonable that they recuperate some of the investment through additional fees. However, keep in mind that many components that are now integrated into the Relational Database Management Systems (RDBMS) started out as separate, additional-cost features.

There are views named *dba_feature_usage_statistics* and *dba_advisor_usage* which record usage of the new features. These reports indicate that the user needs to purchase the license for the additional products. In other words, usage of features like AWR, ASH and ADDM is recorded in the database.

Active Session History

Active Session History is known by its acronym ASH. The ASH consists of session data that is sampled every second and stored in a circular buffer in System Global Areas (SGA). Any session that is connected to the database is considered an active session as long as it is not waiting for an event that belongs to the class of waits defined as idle.

Unlike many of the acronyms in 10g, the "A" in ASH stands for "Active" rather than "Automatic". Tuning with ASH involves using the *v$active_session_history* view and workload repository tables such as *wrh$active_session_history*. The workload repository is discussed in the next section in this chapter. The ASH structures store the history of a session's recent activity, including wait events. The ASH allows analysis of the system performance at the current time as well as in recent history. ASH is designed as a rolling buffer in memory, and earlier information is overwritten when needed. ASH uses memory of the System Global Area (SGA). Figure 8.1 shows the structure of *v$active_session_history*.

```
SQL> desc v$active_session_history
 Name                           Null?      Type
 ------------------------       ----------  -----------------
  SAMPLE_ID                                 NUMBER
  SAMPLE_TIME                               TIMESTAMP(3)
  SESSION_ID                                NUMBER
  SESSION_SERIAL#                           NUMBER
  USER_ID                                   NUMBER
  SQL_ID                                    VARCHAR2(13)
  SQL_CHILD_NUMBER                          NUMBER
  SQL_PLAN_HASH_VALUE                       NUMBER
  SQL_OPCODE                                NUMBER
  SERVICE_HASH                              NUMBER
  SESSION_TYPE                              VARCHAR2(10)
  SESSION_STATE                             VARCHAR2(7)
  QC_SESSION_ID                             NUMBER
  QC_INSTANCE_ID                            NUMBER
  EVENT                                     VARCHAR2(64)
  EVENT_ID                                  NUMBER
  EVENT#                                    NUMBER
  SEQ#                                      NUMBER
  P1                                        NUMBER
  P2                                        NUMBER
  P3                                        NUMBER
  WAIT_TIME                                 NUMBER
  TIME_WAITED                               NUMBER
  CURRENT_OBJ#                              NUMBER
  CURRENT_FILE#                             NUMBER
  CURRENT_BLOCK#                            NUMBER
  PROGRAM                                   VARCHAR2(48)
  MODULE                                    VARCHAR2(48)
  ACTION                                    VARCHAR2(32)
  CLIENT_ID                                 VARCHAR2(64)
```

Figure 8.1 – *Describe of v$active_session_history*

The ASH will be covered in more detail in a later chapter in this book. At that time, the method for using the information contained in the ASH to identify the cause of performance problems will be presented in detail.

Automatic Workload Repository

The *workload repository* consists of the following tables:

- *wrh$_active_session_history*
- *wrh$_bg_event_summary*
- *wrh$_event_name*
- *wrh$_metric_name*
- *wrh$_sessmetric_history*
- *wrh$_sys_time_model*
- *wrh$_sysmetric_history*
- *wrh$_sysmetric_summary*
- *wrh$_sysstat*
- *wrh$_system_event*
- *wrh$_waitclassmetric_history*
- *wrh$_waitstat*

In addition, some of these tables have a counterpart table with the same name and a _bl suffix. These are *baseline* tables and will store statistics about particular areas of the system for a particular point in time. This information is valuable for comparison purposes. If a baseline is taken at a time when performance is good and users subsequently report problems, the DBA can quickly compare data collected during the time of the reported problem to the baseline to see what has changed. Conversely, if the baseline is taken when there are performance problems, then any changes that are made can be compared with the baseline to see if the metrics improve after the change.

Some of the names may have similarity to some of the STATSPACK tables (STATS$). This is because much of the functionality of STATSPACK has been moved into the kernel and is now an integral part of the database. This offers several benefits. First, being part of the kernel code makes these procedures more efficient than they were when STATSPACK was "outside" the kernel. Secondly, the work required to install STATSPACK and configure the required procedures to maintain the data, such as purging old records, is no longer needed because the kernel handles all of these activities by default.

This type of functionality is why Oracle touts the workload repository as one of the 10g features that makes the database easier to manage. However, some of the defaults may not be helpful to DBAs charged with performance enhancement. The various ways an advanced DBA can enhance these features to maximize their benefit are presented in a later chapter.

A quick overview of the *wrh$_active_session_history* table shows that it has a similar structure to the *v$active_session_history* view. The describe of the table is shown in figure 8.2 below.

```
SQL> desc WRH$_ACTIVE_SESSION_HISTORY
 Name                             Null?        Type
 ------------------------------   -----------  ---------------
  SNAP_ID                         NOT NULL     NUMBER
  DBID                            NOT NULL     NUMBER
  INSTANCE_NUMBER                 NOT NULL     NUMBER
  SAMPLE_ID                       NOT NULL     NUMBER
  SAMPLE_TIME                     NOT NULL     TIMESTAMP(3)
  SESSION_ID                      NOT NULL     NUMBER
  SESSION_SERIAL#                              NUMBER
  USER_ID                                      NUMBER
  SQL_ID                                       VARCHAR2(13)
  SQL_CHILD_NUMBER                             NUMBER
  SQL_PLAN_HASH_VALUE                          NUMBER
  SERVICE_HASH                                 NUMBER
  SESSION_TYPE                                 NUMBER
  SQL_OPCODE                                   NUMBER
  QC_SESSION_ID                                NUMBER
  QC_INSTANCE_ID                               NUMBER
  CURRENT_OBJ#                                 NUMBER
  CURRENT_FILE#                                NUMBER
  CURRENT_BLOCK#                               NUMBER
  SEQ#                                         NUMBER
  EVENT_ID                                     NUMBER
```

```
P1                                       NUMBER
P2                                       NUMBER
P3                                       NUMBER
WAIT_TIME                                NUMBER
TIME_WAITED                              NUMBER
PROGRAM                                  VARCHAR2(48)
MODULE                                   VARCHAR2(48)
ACTION                                   VARCHAR2(32)
CLIENT_ID                                VARCHAR2(64)
```

Figure 8.2 – *Describe of wrh$_active_session_history*

Look closely at the differences between the *active_session_history* view in ASH and the workload repository information in the *wrh* table. *v$active_session_history* has three fields that are not in *wrh$_active_session_history*. They are *session_state*, *event*, and *event#*. *event* and *event#* can be derived from other views like *sys.v_$event_name*. *session_state*, on the other hand, represents the current state of the session as to whether it is WAITING or ON CPU.

Conversely, *wrh$_active_session_history* has three fields that are not in *v$active_session_history*. They are *snap_id*, *dbid*, and *instance_number*. These are important for comparing wait events among multiple Real Application Cluster (RAC) nodes.

In order to complete this performance diagnosis, the Oracle database periodically collects information about the database status and the work being processed. Oracle documents say this information is collected once an hour by default; but at least one leading DBA expert indicates that this may happen as often as every 30 minutes.

This data is captured in snapshots somewhat similar to STATSPACK snapshots which are stored in the AWR. The AWR is kept in the SYSAUX tablespace. The SYSAUX tablespace is new to 10g and aids in the reduction of the historical problem of the presence of non-SYSTEM objects in the SYSTEM tablespace. Now the load on the SYSTEM tablespace can be balanced, and fragmentation there can be virtually eliminated since much of the high-activity transactional data is stored by the AWR. These snapshots are maintained at this location for a week by default, but the retention period can be changed by the DBA. After the specified retention period, the snapshots are automatically purged to reduce unneccessary data.

The workload repository is presented in more detail in a subsequent chapter of this book. The information presented in that chapter will illustrate how the information contained in the AWR can be used to identify the cause of performance problems.

Automatic Database Diagnostic Monitor

As indicated by its name, the goal of the Automatic Database Diagnostic Monitor (ADDM) is to automatically monitor and diagnose database problems. The ADDM monitors the data in the AWR and makes tuning recommendations in areas like:

- CPU Utilization

- Connection management

- Parsing activity

- I/O operations

ADDM information is used extensively in the Enterprise Manager Database Diagnostic Pack which provides a graphical front-end that contains information about database performance and recommendations for improvements.

Additionally, ADDM will generate recommendations about sizing certain memory structures. The risks and rewards of using the recommendations generated by the ADDM are presented in later chapters of this book.

The goal of ADDM is to calculate a single throughput metric called DB time, which is the total time spent by the database server in processing user requests. DB time includes the wait time and CPU time of all non-idle user sessions. As presented in a previous chapter in this book, the metric of DB time can be significantly skewed due to events being incorrectly listed as *idle* when they may be significant to the problem at hand. While this can cause problems for the Wait Event performance tuner, a solid understanding of the fundamental architecture of ADDM will allow direct access to more granular information and the skewing can be avoided or minimized.

The key views used for ADDM are *v$sess_time_model* (Figure 8.3) and *v$sys_time_model* (Figure 8.4) as shown below.

```
SQL> desc v$sess_time_model
 Name                              Null?       Type
 -------------------------------  ----------  ----------------
 SID                                          NUMBER
 STAT_ID                                      NUMBER
 STAT_NAME                                    VARCHAR2(64)
 VALUE                                        NUMBER
```
Figure 8.3 – *Describe of v$sess_time_model*

```
SQL> desc v$sys_time_model
 Name                              Null?       Type
 -------------------------------  ----------  ----------------
 STAT_ID                                      NUMBER
 STAT_NAME                                    VARCHAR2(64)
 VALUE                                        NUMBER
```
Figure 8.4 – *Describe of v$sys_time_model*

Notice the similarity to the *v$sesstat* and *v$sysstat* views which contain database statistics at the session and system level. These new *time model* views contain the same type of information on either a system-wide basis (*v$sys_time_model*) or a session level basis (*v$sess_time_model*). Figure 8.5 shows a sample of the types of statistics maintained in these views.

```
STAT_NAME                                                  VALUE
---------------------------------------------------   ---------
Db time                                                 46618362
DB CPU                                                   7085917
background elapsed time                                 41476062
background cpu time                                      8064729
sequence load elapsed                                      45777
parse time elapsed                                      14927310
hard parse elapsed time                                 13987060
sql execute elapsed time                                44480913
connection management call elapsed time                  1244837
failed parse elapsed time                                      0
failed parse (out of shared memory) elapsed time               0
hard parse (sharing criteria) elapsed time                  2993
hard parse (bind mismatch) elapsed time                     1217
PL/SQL execution elapsed time                             687309
inbound PL/SQL rpc elapsed time                                0
PL/SQL compilation elapsed time                          1974167
Java execution elapsed time                              3512918
```

Figure 8.5 – *Sample data in time_model views*

Advice Please

Other views that are important for ADDM are those that start with *dba_advisor*. Some of these views are described briefly in Figure 8.6 below. Additional information on using ADDM is covered in a later chapter in this book..

VIEW NAME	DESCRIPTION
dba_advisor_definitions	List of the names of the advisors
dba_advisor_usage	Tracks number and last time advisors were run
dba_advisor_log	History of *dba_advisor* executions with status
dba_advisor_findings	Results from the advisor reports

Figure 8.6 – *Some of the views used by ADDM advisors*

One might ask: What are these advisors anyway? The *dba_advisor_definitions* view is a great place to start looking for this the answer to this question. Presented in Figure 8.7, is a list of the advisor names obtained from this view.

```
ADVISOR_NAME
------------------------
ADDM
SQL Access Advisor
Undo Advisor
SQL Tuning Advisor
Segment Advisor
SQL Workload Manager
Tune MView
```

Figure 8.7 – *List of advisors*

"Ms. Jones, could you please bring me my list of advisors."

There are alternatives to these advisors. Two of the alternatives are trial and error, which works with varying degrees of effectiveness, and the application of methods discussed in this book to achieve effective performance enhancements. Another alternative is the purchase of third party products, although the ADDM advisors have some advantages over the competition.

First, the ADDM advisors are from the same company that produces the RDBMS software so the development staff had access to proprietary documentation that should enhance overall functionality. Secondly, the ADDM advisors are more likely to be kept current when the database software is upgraded, whereas third party tools are, by definition, "playing catch-up". Finally, the ADDM advisors offer relief to the overburdened DBA who is overwhelmed with databases and options for tuning. In many cases, DBAs are simply trying to maintain databases much like a juggling act that is only one ball drop away from getting out of hand. These advisors act as assistants to help narrow down the areas that are in critical need of attention. This assistance frees the DBA from having to wading through all of the possible areas of concern and go straight to addressing the most critical areas.

One of the advisors is the SQL Tuning Advisor. This advisor provides tuning advice when provided with a poorly performing SQL statement. This can make the tuning process much simpler because the DBA is no longer required to manually perform an explain plan and test different scenarios. This process can also be more effective since the advisor is using the cost based optimizer (CBO) to obtain the tuning advice, and the CBO is the component that will be responsible for the eventual execution of the SQL statement.

Many advisors use the concept of wait classes to classify various events into common groups. The following section will address these wait classes.

Wait Classes

The concept of a class is not new. The class of waits that have traditionally been called "idle waits" was presented earlier in this book. Expert DBAs have written scripts and tools to aggregate specific wait events to certain categories like I/O or CPU. These are all examples of classes. The wait interface in Oracle10g now includes wait classes. The eight classes that have been defined are:

- Commit
- Concurrency
- Configuration
- Idle
- Network
- Other
- System I/O
- User I/O

The danger associated with events being improperly classified still applies. For example, SQL*Net waits have traditionally been classified as idle events, but in many cases actually represent a root cause problem that needs to be addressed in order to alleviate a performance problem.

In spite of this danger, wait classes hold great promise in terms of making tuning simpler for the novice DBA. However, more experienced DBAs may prefer to identify the problem by determining that the slow process is waiting on db file scattered read rather than learning from the advisor that the slow process is waiting on something in the User I/O class. The ability to "drill down" and discover not only that the main wait event is db file scattered read, but that it is reading file #4, block 3892 is critical for in-depth problem solving.

The next section presents the views that use wait classes as well as some of the other new views available in 10g.

"It's possible we may have waited too long for this guy"

Wait Class v$views

v$system_wait_class

This view allows the DBA to look at the time totals for each registered wait class in the entire instance. The related view *v$session_wait_class* tracks the same information down to the user SID and Serial#. It may be helpful to think of these as a summary of *v$system_event* and *v$session_event* as they sum up the values available and group them by the pre-defined classes.

v$event_histogram

Another of the new views provided in 10g is *v$event_histogram*. Many DBAs are familiar with the concept of a histogram from either statistics classes or earlier versions of Oracle where

---

histogram data that allowed the CBO to get a better understanding of the data distribution could be collected. For example, if a small company with 10 employees that had been employed for 10 years recently hired a new person, the *hire_date* field would be highly skewed. Any query that used *hire_date* as a selective criterion would be more effective if this field had a histogram.

The *v$event_histogram* view is similar to index histograms in that it conveys information about the distribution of wait events. It allows the comparison of the frequency and "weight" of a wait event. This allows the DBA to see if the normal wait time is high, or if there are a few outlier events where the wait time was significant. The query *db_file_wait_histograms.sql* can be used to look at events relating to database file activity (i.e. db file sequential/scattered/parallel read/write). This example can be modified to retrieve any information of interest by simply changing the where clause.

🖫 db_file_wait_histograms.sql

```
-- ****************************************************
-- Copyright © 2003 by Rampant TechPress
-- This script is free for non-commercial purposes
-- with no warranties.  Use at your own risk.
--
-- To license this script for a commercial purpose,
-- contact info@rampant.cc
-- ****************************************************

/* db_file_wait_histograms.sql */
column event form a30
column wait_time_milli HEAD "WAIT|TIME|(ms)"
column wait_count HEAD "WAIT|COUNT"

select
   event,
   wait_time_milli,
   wait_count
from
   v$event_histogram
where
   event like 'db%';
```

```
SQL> @db_file_wait_histograms

                                        WAIT
                                        TIME          WAIT
EVENT                                   (ms)          COUNT
--------------------------------------- ------------  ------------
db file sequential read                    1              5015
db file sequential read                    2                90
db file sequential read                    4               126
db file sequential read                    8               552
db file sequential read                   16              1432
db file sequential read                   32              1020
db file sequential read                   64               487
db file sequential read                  128                80
db file sequential read                  256                14
db file scattered read                     1               687
db file scattered read                     2                13
db file scattered read                     4                38
db file scattered read                     8                71
db file scattered read                    16               237
db file scattered read                    32               194
db file scattered read                    64                67
db file scattered read                   128                33
db file scattered read                   256                15
db file scattered read                   512                 3
db file parallel write                     1              3199
```

Figure 8.8 – *Output from db_file_wait_histograms.sql*

Figure 8.8 shows the results of *db_file_wait_histograms.sql*. Examination of these results shows several things:

- Never since this database was started has a *db_file_parallel_write* taken more than 1 millisecond (ms.), even though this operation has been performed 3,199 times.

- The majority of the *db_file_sequential_read* operations (5,015 ~ 57%) have taken less than 1 ms.

- A measurable amount of the *db_file_sequential_read* operations (2,452 ~ 28%) have taken more than 8 ms and less than 32 ms.

This type of analysis is helpful when there is a need to identify the extent and magnitude of a given problem.

v$eventmetric

This view displays the values of the wait event metrics for the most recent interval. The structure of this view is shown in figure 8.9.

```
SQL> desc v$eventmetric
 Name                          Null?       Type
 ----------------------------- ----------- --------
 BEGIN_TIME                                DATE
 END_TIME                                  DATE
 INTSIZE_CSEC                              NUMBER
 EVENT#                                    NUMBER
 EVENT_ID                                  NUMBER
 NUM_SESS_WAITING                          NUMBER
 TIME_WAITED                               NUMBER
 WAIT_COUNT                                NUMBER
```

Figure 8.9 – *Describe v$eventmetric*

This is a short-term view and only stores information for about the past minute. The exact duration of the data is shown in the *INTSIZE_CSEC* field, which represents the number of centiseconds in this interval. In the example shown in Figure 8.10, on the interval on the Linux test system is 6018 cs, which when rounded to the nearest second equates to one minute and two seconds. This data can be obtained by running *eventmetric.sql* available in the code depot.

💾 eventmetric.sql

```
-- ****************************************************
-- Copyright © 2003 by Rampant TechPress
-- This script is free for non-commercial purposes
-- with no warranties.  Use at your own risk.
--
-- To license this script for a commercial purpose,
-- contact info@rampant.cc
-- ****************************************************

/* eventmetric.sql */
column INTSIZE_CSEC format 99999 heading INTERVAL|SIZE
column EVENT#  format 9999
column NUM_SESS_WAITING format 9999 heading NUMBER|SESSIONS|WAITING
```

```
column TIME_WAITED format 999999 heading TIME|WAITED
column WAIT_COUNT format 9999 heading WAIT|COUNT
select
    to_char(begin_time, 'DD/MON/YYYY HH24:MI:SS') "BEGIN",
    to_char(end_time, 'DD/MON/YYYY HH24:MI:SS') "END",
    intsize_csec,
    event#,
    event_id,
    num_sess_waiting,
    time_waited,
    wait_count
from
    v$eventmetric
where
    num_sess_waiting > 0
or
    time_waited > 0
or
    wait_count > 0
order by
    time_waited DESC;
```

BEGIN	END	INTERNAL SIZE	EVENT#	EVENT_ID	NUMBER SESSIONS WAITING	TIME WAITED	WAIT COUNT
07/MAY/2004 22:17:32	07/MAY/2004 22:18:33	6018	33	866018717	7	40748	168
07/MAY/2004 22:17:32	07/MAY/2004 22:18:33	6018	621	299395645	1	6000	2
07/MAY/2004 22:17:32	07/MAY/2004 22:18:33	6018	12	3539483025	1	5877	21
07/MAY/2004 22:17:32	07/MAY/2004 22:18:33	6018	523	3618703989	0	5861	2
07/MAY/2004 22:17:32	07/MAY/2004 22:18:33	6018	524	4090013609	0	5860	1
07/MAY/2004 22:17:32	07/MAY/2004 22:18:33	6018	592	1421975091	2	5648	12
07/MAY/2004 22:17:32	07/MAY/2004 22:18:33	6018	187	2779959231	0	2465	236
07/MAY/2004 22:17:32	07/MAY/2004 22:18:33	6018	499	1242501677	0	290	10
07/MAY/2004 22:17:32	07/MAY/2004 22:18:33	6018	173	4078387448	0	5	19
07/MAY/2004 22:17:32	07/MAY/2004 22:18:33	6018	450	1403232821	1	0	0
07/MAY/2004 22:17:32	07/MAY/2004 22:18:33	6018	608	2007546364	1	0	0
07/MAY/2004 22:17:32	07/MAY/2004 22:18:33	6018	588	2067390145	0	0	12

Figure 8.10 – *Sample v$eventmetric data*

What can be learned from this view? In some ways, this view is similar to the *v$session_wait* view, in that it maintains recent wait information. However, it is different in that this view stores system-wide information and instead of only storing current waits, it stores approximately one minute's worth of history. The difference between current information and one minute of history seems small, but it becomes much easier to monitor ongoing sessions. The DBA could, for instance, have a procedure that captures *v$eventmetric* data every minute. Due to the history collected with *v$eventmetric*, significantly more data

Wait Class v$views

would be captured than if only *v$session_wait* data was captured at the same interval.

In the example above at the end of the past one-minute (60.2 seconds), there were seven sessions waiting for event #33. These sessions had accumulated 40748 cs, which is an average of 58.2 seconds per session. On average, each of these seven sessions spent most of that minute waiting. There may have been sessions that ended or became inactive before the end of this timing interval, but this view only reports the number of sessions active at the end of the interval.

v$event_name can be used to identify event #33 by using *event_info.sql.* This script will generate the data information shown in figure 8.11.

💾 event_info.sql

```
-- *******************************************
-- Copyright © 2003 by Rampant TechPress
-- This script is free for non-commercial purposes
-- with no warranties.  Use at your own risk.
--
-- To license this script for a commercial purpose,
-- contact info@rampant.cc
-- *******************************************

/* event_info.sql */
column event# format 9999
column name format a35
column wait_class_id format 99999999999
column wait_class format a15
select
   event#,
   name ,
   wait_class_id,
   wait_class
from
   v$event_name
where
   event# = &event;
```

```
EVENT# NAME                              WAIT_CLASS_ID  WAIT_CLASS
------ ---------------------------       -------------  ----------
    33 rdbms ipc message                    2723168908  Idle
```

Figure 8.11 – *Sample v$event_name data*

According to prevailing wisdom, "rdbms ipc message" event is a non-issue. Therefore, in this example, the *v$eventmetric* view is reporting a non-problem as the event which is having the greatest impact on database performance. This highlights one of the drawbacks to this view which is that it contains only aggregate statistics rather than detailed data by session. It is entirely possible that the largest source of system-wide time use is something completely different than what is causing a specific user to call and report a "system slowness" problem.

v$waitclassmetric

v$waitclassmetric is a rollup of *v$eventmetric*. Recalling the earlier discussion regarding the concept of *wait classes*, it is apparent that this is one of the ways Oracle is attempting to make database performance tuning easier, particularly for the less-experienced DBA For the more experienced DBA, the wait classes might provide a quick health check; however, the resolution of a specific problem may be most effective with more granular detail.

By querying *v$waitclassmetric*, the biggest area of concern can be quickly identified. *waitclassmetric.sql* is a sample query that can be used for the identification of such areas of concern and produces a report similar to the one shown in Figure 8.12.

🖫 **waitclassmetric.sql**

```
-- To license this script for a commercial purpose,
-- contact info@rampant.cc
-- *************************************************

/* waitclassmetric.sql */
column INTSIZE_CSEC format 99999 heading INTERVAL|SIZE
column WAIT_CLASS# format 99999 heading WAIT|CLASS
column DBTIME_IN_WAIT format 999999 heading "DBTIME|IN WAIT"
column AVERAGE_WAITER_COUNT format 9999 heading "AVG #|WAITERS"
column TIME_WAITED format 999999 heading TIME|WAITED
column WAIT_COUNT format 99999 heading WAIT|COUNT
select
   to_char(begin_time, 'DD/MON/YYYY HH24:MI:SS') "BEGIN",
   to_char(end_time, 'DD/MON/YYYY HH24:MI:SS') "END",
   intsize_csec,
   wait_class#,
   wait_class_id,
   average_waiter_count,
   time_waited,
   wait_count
from
   v$waitclassmetric
where
   average_waiter_count > 0
or
   time_waited > 0
or
   wait_count > 0
order by
   time_waited DESC;
```

BEGIN	END	INTERVAL SIZE	WAIT CLASS	WAIT_CLASS_ID	AVG # WAITERS	TIME WAITED	WAIT COUNT
08/MAY/2004 15:56:17	08/MAY/2004 15:57:19	6018	6	2723168908	14	85461	199
08/MAY/2004 15:56:17	08/MAY/2004 15:57:19	6018	9	4108307767	0	6	32
08/MAY/2004 15:56:17	08/MAY/2004 15:57:19	6018	7	2000153315	0	0	2

Figure 8.12 – *Sample v$waitclassmetric data*

The DBA might be interested in seeing what wait classes 6, 7 and 9 represent. Querying the *v$system_wait_class* view is one way to identify what the wait classes represent. This view has a historical rollup for the entire time the instance has been up, but it also provides a way to change *wait_class#* into the name of that class. *wait_class_info.sql* is a simple query that could easily be plugged into *waitclassmetric.sql* to include the name of the wait class in addition to the number. Sample output of this script is shown in Figure 8.13.

```
--  ****************************************************
-- Copyright © 2003 by Rampant TechPress
-- This script is free for non-commercial purposes
-- with no warranties.  Use at your own risk.
--
-- To license this script for a commercial purpose,
-- contact info@rampant.cc
--  ****************************************************

select
   wait_class# ,
   wait_class
from
   v$system_wait_class
where
   wait_class# in (&class);
```

```
  WAIT
 CLASS WAIT_CLASS
------- ----------
      6 Idle
      7 Network
      9 System I/O
```

Figure 8.13 – *More information on Wait Classes*

Conclusion

Some of these views offer only current and recent history. Some offer a longer history in the *related _history* tables. Additional views as well as sample queries that take advantage of the data they are storing are presented in later chapters in this book.

This chapter introduced many of the Wait Interface enhancements that are found in 10g. The following chapters will go into more detail about other important enhancements. These chapters will show ways that Oracle10g enhancements can be incorporated into the tuning process.

Active Session History and Automated Work Repository

Active Session History

Introduction

As mentioned in the last chapter, tuning with Active Session History (ASH) involves use of the *v$active_session_history* view. This view contains information on sessions that are active when the sampling takes place. This sampling occurs every second, and the sampled data is kept in a buffer in the System Global Area (SGA). This buffer is overwritten for space, as necessary. Any connected and active session that is waiting for a non-idle event is included in this sampled data. Sessions using CPU at the time of sampling are included since CPU usage is not considered idle time.

Active Session History vs. Automated Workload Repository

v$active_session_history is also part of the Automatic Workload Repository (AWR), which is covered in more detail later in this chapter. This view is the source for some of the longer-term information that is kept in the AWR. The next section will demonstrate how *v$active_session_history* can be used to identify and resolve an on-going performance problem. A later section in this chapter will explain how to use the AWR to identify a performance problem that either took place in the past or is intermittent in nature.

Additionally, *v$active_session_history* is a primary source of data for the Automatic Database Diagnostic Monitor (ADDM). The ADDM is covered in more detail in another chapter in this book.

Relationships

In order to use ASH, it is necessary to understand the layout of the views. Refer to Figure 8.1 in the previous chapter for details on the structure of *v$active_session_history*. Figure 9.1 below shows the connection between the *v$session* data, a key ASH view called *v$active_session_history*, and the AWR structure *wrh$_active_session_history*. The underlined fields can be used to join the other views to gather the specific information needed to diagnose performance problems.

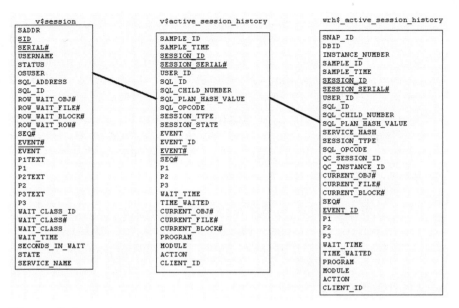

v$session	v$active_session_history	wrh$_active_session_history
SADDR	SAMPLE_ID	SNAP_ID
SID	SAMPLE_TIME	DBID
SERIAL#	SESSION_ID	INSTANCE_NUMBER
USERNAME	SESSION_SERIAL#	SAMPLE_ID
STATUS	USER_ID	SAMPLE_TIME
OSUSER	SQL_ID	SESSION_ID
SQL_ADDRESS	SQL_CHILD_NUMBER	SESSION_SERIAL#
SQL_ID	SQL_PLAN_HASH_VALUE	USER_ID
ROW_WAIT_OBJ#	SQL_OPCODE	SQL_ID
ROW_WAIT_FILE#	SESSION_TYPE	SQL_CHILD_NUMBER
ROW_WAIT_BLOCK#	SESSION_STATE	SQL_PLAN_HASH_VALUE
ROW_WAIT_ROW#	EVENT	SERVICE_HASH
SEQ#	EVENT_ID	SESSION_TYPE
EVENT#	EVENT#	SQL_OPCODE
EVENT	SEQ#	QC_SESSION_ID
P1TEXT	P1	QC_INSTANCE_ID
P1	P2	CURRENT_OBJ#
P2TEXT	P3	CURRENT_FILE#
P2	WAIT_TIME	CURRENT_BLOCK#
P3TEXT	TIME_WAITED	SEQ#
P3	CURRENT_OBJ#	EVENT_ID
WAIT_CLASS_ID	CURRENT_FILE#	P1
WAIT_CLASS#	CURRENT_BLOCK#	P2
WAIT_CLASS	PROGRAM	P3
WAIT_TIME	MODULE	WAIT_TIME
SECONDS_IN_WAIT	ACTION	TIME_WAITED
STATE	CLIENT_ID	PROGRAM
SERVICE_NAME		MODULE
		ACTION
		CLIENT_ID

Figure 9.1 – *Relationships among v$session and other structures*

Due to the volume of data found in *v$active_session_history* during times of heavy activity, not all of the data is stored in the AWR tables. This is because the "dirty read" mechanism reads data even though it may belong to an in-process transaction, which allows the impact on the database to be negligible. In spite of the fact that the AWR does not store all of the data from *v$active_session_history*, enough data is collected to allow the AWR information to be statistically accurate and useful for historical review.

How to Use ASH

The primary reason for using the current ASH tables like *v$active_session_history* and *v$session* is troubleshooting a problem that is currently going on. In this case, the use of the term history in *v$active_session_history* may be misleading since the history is time-limited. This time limitation is directly related to the amount of data stored there. If the database is active; the time that data is kept in the history will be shorter, and if the database is idle, the data will be kept longer.

v$session_wait can be queried to get information on which sessions are currently waiting. The information available includes:

- *SID*
- *EVENT*
- *P1TEXT*
- *P1*
- *P2TEXT*
- *P2*
- *P3TEXT*
- *P3*
- *WAIT_TIME*
- *SECONDS_IN_WAIT*
- *STATE*

If *v$active_session_history* is queried instead, the TEXT information for the *P1*, *P2* and *P3* fields is lost, but *CURRENT_OBJ#*, *CURRENT_FILE#* and *CURRENT_BLOCK#* are gained. These three new fields allow the querying of *v$session* using *row_wait_obj#, row_wait_file#* and *row_wait_block#*. Using a query like *session_ash.sql*, which joins *v$session* and *v$active_session_history*, the *v$session* information can be reviewed for sessions that are in the ASH views.

session_ash.sql

```
-- ****************************************************
-- Copyright © 2003 by Rampant TechPress
-- This script is free for non-commercial purposes
-- with no warranties.  Use at your own risk.
--
-- To license this script for a commercial purpose,
-- contact info@rampant.cc
-- ****************************************************

/* session_ash.sql */
/* This reports information on object being waited on */
/* when the wait is I/O related */
select a.CURRENT_OBJ#, a.CURRENT_FILE#, a.CURRENT_BLOCK#,
b.SID, b.SERIAL#, b.USERNAME, b.OSUSER
from v$active_session_history a, v$session b
where
a.CURRENT_OBJ# = b.row_wait_obj#
and a.CURRENT_FILE# = b.row_wait_file#
and a.CURRENT_BLOCK# = b.row_wait_block#
and a.SESSION_SERIAL# = b.SERIAL#
and a.SESSION_ID = b.SID;
```

CURRENT_OBJ#	CURRENT_FILE#	CURRENT_BLOCK#	SID	SERIAL#	USERNAME	OSUSER
49807	4	1547	91	5	WEBBER	oracle
49807	4	2046	92	10	WEBBER	oracle
49807	4	1963	106	9	WEBBER	oracle
49807	4	2046	107	5	WEBBER	oracle
49807	4	145	95	3	WEBBER	oracle

Figure 9.2 – *Sample of session_ash.sql showing user session information*

More importantly, by joining with *v$session*, the *USERNAME* and *OSUSER* can be seen as well as the display of the *SQL_ID,* so the actual SQL statement being run can be identified. With the information provided above, the DBA is able to take the object ID from the *CURRECT_OBJ#* field and identify the specific object that is being waited on. In figure 9.2, the five sessions listed are all waiting for object number 49807. *find_object_name.sql* can take that object number and identify the owner and name of the object as shown in figure 9.3.

```
-- *****************************************************
-- Copyright © 2003 by Rampant TechPress
-- This script is free for non-commercial purposes
-- with no warranties.  Use at your own risk.
--
-- To license this script for a commercial purpose,
-- contact info@rampant.cc
-- *****************************************************

/* find_object_name.sql */
column OWNER format a10
column OBJECT_NAME format a25
column OBJECT_ID format 999999
column OBJECT_TYPE format a25
select
   OWNER,
   OBJECT_NAME,
   OBJECT_ID,
   OBJECT_TYPE,
   CREATED
from
   dba_objects
where
   OBJECT_ID = &object_id;
```

```
Enter value for object_id: 49807
old  10:    OBJECT_ID = &object_id
new  10:    OBJECT_ID = 49807

OWNER       OBJECT_NAM OBJECT_ID OBJECT_TYP CREATED
---------- ---------- --------- ---------- ---------
WEBBER      HITS           49807 TABLE      06-MAY-04
```

Figure 9.3 – *Sample of find_object_name.sql*

Figure 9.3 shows the object that is causing the waits as identified by *session_ash.sql* is owned by the user WEBBER and is a single object. Further research, as shown in Figure 9.4 generated by *ash_top_10.sql* below, shows this user to be performing queries that are causing unnecessary full table scans. An appropriately placed function-based index would dramatically reduce the load, and therefore wait time, on this object. This information may not be helpful if all of the queries are looking for a lower-case value. The query that generated figure 9.4 is explained in more detail below.

```
                                                                          SESSION
TRUNC(SAM   SID SERIAL# USERNAME  EVENT                     P1      P2 WAIT_TIME TIME_WAITED STATE
--------- ----- ------- --------- ------------------------- ------- -------- --------- ----------- ---------
SQL_TEXT
-------------------------------------------------------------------------------------------------
25-MAY-04   95       3 WEBBER     read by other session          4    2395     11166           0 ON CPU
SELECT COUNT(*) FROM HITS WHERE UPPER(AREA) != 'a'

25-MAY-04  107       5 WEBBER     db file sequential read        1    7573         0      177258 WAITING
BEGIN DBMS_OUTPUT.DISABLE; END;

25-MAY-04  106       9 WEBBER     read by other session          4    2395         0       11713 WAITING
SELECT COUNT(*) FROM HITS WHERE UPPER(AREA) != 'a'
```

Figure 9.4 – *Digging in to cause of slowness*

ash_top_10.sql is a query of *v$active_session_history* joined with *dba_users* to get username and *v$sql* to obtain the SQL statement. Figure 9.5 shows some of the records from a sample system.

🖫 ash_top_10.sql

```
-- ****************************************************
-- Copyright © 2003 by Rampant TechPress
-- This script is free for non-commercial purposes
-- with no warranties.  Use at your own risk.
--
-- To license this script for a commercial purpose,
-- contact info@rampant.cc
-- ****************************************************

/* ash_top_10.sql */
column sql_text format a120 WRAP
column session_id form 9999 head SID
column session_serial# form 9999 head SERIAL#
column sql_text format a120 WRAP
column sample_time format a10
column username format a10
column session_state format a10 head SESSION|STATE
column event format a30
column p1 format 999999999
column p2 format 9999999
column p3 format 9999999

select
   trunc(SAMPLE_TIME),
   SESSION_ID,
   SESSION_SERIAL#,
   USERNAME,
```

```
   EVENT,
   P1,
   P2,
   P3,
   WAIT_TIME,
   TIME_WAITED,
   SESSION_STATE,
   SQL_TEXT
from
   v$active_session_history a,
   dba_users b,
   v$sql c
where
   a.user_id = b.user_id
and
   a.sql_id = c.sql_id
and
   rownum < 11
and
   a.user_id != 0
order by
   wait_time DESC,
   time_waited DESC;
```

```
                                                                    WAIT
TRUNC(SAM  SID SERIAL# USERNAME   EVENT                     P1          P2    TIME TIME_WAITED SESSION
---------  ---- ------- ---------- ------------------------- ----------- ----------- ------ ----------- -------
SQL_TEXT
-----------------------------------------------------------------------------------------------------------
17-MAY-04   89     41 WEBBER     db file sequential read           1     11940 22721          0 ON CPU
SELECT ATTRIBUTE,SCOPE,NUMERIC_VALUE,CHAR_VALUE,DATE_VALUE FROM SYSTEM.PRODUCT_PRIVS WHERE (UPPER('SQL*Plus') LIKE UPPER
(PRODUCT)) AND (UPPER(USER) LIKE USERID)

17-MAY-04   91      2 WEBBER     enq: HW - contention     1213661190      4     0     291033 WAITING
insert into mktrptlog values (  to_date('17-MAY-04 08:45:05pm','DD-MON-YY HH:MI:SSam'),to_date('17-MAY-04 08:45:05pm','
DD-MON-YY HH:MI:SSam'))

17-MAY-04   93    366 WEBBER     enq: HW - contention     1213661190      4     0     281147 WAITING
insert into mktrptlog values (  to_date('17-MAY-04 08:45:05pm','DD-MON-YY HH:MI:SSam'),to_date('17-MAY-04 08:45:05pm','
DD-MON-YY HH:MI:SSam'))
```

Figure 9.5 – *ASH Top 10 sample report*

When reviewing Figure 9.5, it is important to remember the difference between *WAIT_TIME* and *TIME_WAITED*. *WAIT_TIME* is the total time waited by the session for the event listed, if the session was on the CPU (i.e. *SESSION_STATE* = "*ON CPU*") when sampled the last time.

If *WAIT_TIME* is 0, the session currently has a *SESSION_STATE* of "*WAITING*", and the event listed in the *EVENT* field is the last event that was waited for before this sample. *TIME_WAITED* is the amount of time that the session waited for the event listed in the *EVENT* field.

If *WAIT_TIME* is greater than 0, the session currently has a *SESSION_STATE* of "*ON CPU*", and the event listed in the *EVENT* field is the event that was last waited for before this sample. *TIME_WAITED* will be 0. *TIME_WAITED* will only contain a value when waits are occurring at the instant the sample is taken.

For example, this means that if *WAIT_TIME* in one row is 2, then the *SESSION_STATE* will be "*ON CPU*" and then *TIME_WAITED* will be 0. The 2 in *WAIT_TIME* represents the time spent waiting the last time it waited before the current time on the CPU.

In this script, data was sorted by *WAIT_TIME* first and *TIME_WAITED* second. This is simply because it will first list everything that is currently using CPU. The information provided is for the most recent wait event, which is the focus of this book.

Automatic Workload Repository

Introduction

ASH keeps current and recent information on the work a database is performing. In earlier Oracle versions, tracking historical data longer than a few seconds or minutes would require the choice of one of the following available options:

- a custom-written procedure
- STATSPACK or its predecessor UTLESTAT/UTLESTAT
- an application from a third party.

With 10g, the Automatic Workload Repository (AWR) incorporates much of STATSPACK into the database internals.

STATSPACK is in wide use and is still available for 10g. In addition, many books have been written regarding the use of STATSPACK to solve database performance problems. With these factors and the knowledge that already exists for many DBAs, one might ask why bother looking into the AWR. Indeed, for some DBAs it may make sense to continue to use STATSPACK either for financial reasons, recalling the licensing information discussed earlier in this book or simply to avoid the learning curve associated with effective use of the AWR.

Even if another primary performance tuning tool is chosen, this section on the AWR may help the DBA should circumstances change. If the AWR is chosen as the primary tuning tool, this section provides a good start on the road to understanding the components of this tool, and how those components can help solve performance problems.

The AWR forms the foundation for self-tuning features in 10g

Since the AWR forms the foundation for the self-tuning features found in Oracle10g, and even if getting involved in heavy-duty tuning is not planned, an understanding of this information is important since it will facilitate a better understanding of what is incorporated into self-tuning. Even if the plan is to have the Oracle database tune itself, the DBA may want to change the way it gathers and stores the data.

How to Use the AWR

To get started with the AWR, nothing needs to be installed other than the Oracle10g database. This is one feature of the AWR that is a benefit over STATSPACK. The AWR automatically collects data as soon as Oracle10g is installed and running. With STATSPACK, the DBA determined the frequency of data collection and then scheduled a job to run at the appropriate interval to gather data. With the AWR, the documentation states that these collections are done every 30 minutes, but the frequency can be modified by the user. The resulting data is stored in the AWR for seven days, by default, after which the data is automatically purged.

Based on user testing, it appears that the default of 30 minute snapshot intervals, as stated by the documentation, may not be correct. In some cases, the interval appeared to be 60 minutes rather than 30 minutes. A later section will provide a method for determining the actual "default" sampling interval. Additionally, instructions on how to change these defaults are also included. Every DBA should assess the frequency of the snapshots as well as the length of time they are retained and adjust the AWR settings accordingly.

This data is gathered and populated into the AWR by the new 10g MMON and MMNL (MMON Lite) processes. MMON is also responsible for issuing alerts when there are metrics that exceed thresholds.

As far as using this data, this book will only address the use of scripts to access the AWR data. Oracle Enterprise Manager (OEM) can also be used to access the data, but OEM is a topic unto itself. In this book, this topic is limited to the non-gui tools or direct access to the data dictionary objects.

Since nothing extra needs to be installed, the data tables that support this feature are up for discussion. The AWR contains a number of new tables in the data dictionary. These are:

- *dba_hist_active_sess_history*

Automatic Workload Repository   **219**

- *dba_hist_baseline*

- *dba_hist_database_instance*

- *dba_hist_snapshot*

- *dba_hist_sql_plan*

- *dba_hist_wr_control*

The structure of *dba_hist_active_sess_history* is essentially the same as *v$active_session_history* with the exception of the additional fields at the top with which to track the snapshot details for when and where the data was collected. This view actually represents the data that is periodically collected from *v$active_session_history* in a manner similar to the way STATSPACK collects data.

Reports

Several similarities between AWR and STATSPACK have been presented and this section will mention some more. In Chapter 7, the basic report that Oracle provides with STATSPACK as generated by the *spreport.sql* script was presented. Oracle has provided similar functionality with the AWR in the form of *awrrpt.sql* and *awrrpti.sql*. *awrrpt.sql* is very similar to *spreport.sql*, and *awrrpti.sql* adds the functionality of reporting on a specific database when data for multiple databases are stored in the same repository.

awrrpt.sql provides information on the time range covered by the report, the host, the instance, and the database name as well as the set of metrics and ratios intended to measure database health at a glance. This new report shows the features in the Top 5 Timed Events where there is a new column called Wait Class.

Manually analyzing this report involves some of the procedures used when analyzing the STATSPACK report, so intricate detail will not be included on that subject in this section. As Oracle10g gains exposure, the availability of other options is expected. Vendor solutions and free websites are two potential sources for support of these files.

Baselines

A baseline is simply a snapshot at a point in time. Database information can be compared against a baseline to determine if things have gotten better, worse, or stayed the same. Baselines can be created with the *dbms_workload_repository.create_baseline* procedure. Some DBAs might currently be experiencing DBA nirvana where all of the users are happy and engaged in DBA worship. First, these DBAs should enjoy it while it lasts. Secondly, these DBAs should create a baseline so when the users start throwing stones, data will be available for comparing the new performance metrics to the ones when things were good. With any luck, those DBAs will find the cause of the problem and be quickly back on the road to happiness.

For everyone but that lucky DBA, a baseline should be taken as soon as the system is stable. For a typical Online Transaction Processing (OLTP) system, this stable time may fall on Monday at mid-day since users in earlier time zones have been at work for several hours and users in later time zones have not yet taken lunch. On Mondays, many workloads will have a weekend backlog which means that the load will be somewhat higher than that for the rest of the week. After analyzing this report and making changes which have been properly vetted through the TEST and DEVELOPMENT environments, an additional baseline can be taken at the same time on another Monday and a statistical analysis performed to determine what has changed, whether it is a good change and if the change is what had been expected.

After taking a baseline of a two-hour window of work from one day and another from the next day, the *dba_hist_baseline* will look something like Figure 9.6. Notice that the baseline names in this example are simply the date of the baseline in yyyy-mm-dd order. This makes sorting very easy using only the *baseline_name* field. However, *baseline name* is merely a text field and a baseline called "fred and ginger dance partners" could just as easily be created.

```
BASELINE_ID BASELINE_NAME
----------- --------------
          1 2004_06_06
          2 2004_06_07
```

Figure 9.6 – *Baseline Names*

These baselines are created using data captured by the AWR. Before running the command to create a baseline, it is a good idea to know which snapshots are from which times. The following script, *awr_list_snaps.sql*, can help with that. Figure 9.7 shows this script in action.

🖫 awr_list_snaps.sql

```
-- *************************************************
-- Copyright © 2003 by Rampant TechPress
-- This script is free for non-commercial purposes
-- with no warranties.  Use at your own risk.
--
-- To license this script for a commercial purpose,
-- contact info@rampant.cc
-- *************************************************

/* awr_list_snaps.sql */
column SNAP_ID format 999999
column BEGIN_INTERVAL_TIME format a25
column END_INTERVAL_TIME format a25
column SNAP_LEVEL format 99 head LEVEL

select
   snap_id,
   begin_interval_time,
```

Oracle Wait Event Tuning

```
      end_interval_time,
      snap_level
from
      dba_hist_snapshot
order by 1;
```

```
SNAP_ID BEGIN_INTERVAL_TIME          END_INTERVAL_TIME            LEVEL
------- ------------------------     ------------------------     -----
    763 06-JUN-04 07.00.11.463 PM    06-JUN-04 08.00.34.741 PM        1
    764 06-JUN-04 08.00.34.741 PM    06-JUN-04 09.00.58.016 PM        1
    765 06-JUN-04 09.00.58.016 PM    06-JUN-04 10.00.19.916 PM        1
    788 07-JUN-04 07.00.27.141 PM    07-JUN-04 07.00.37.263 PM        1
    789 07-JUN-04 07.00.37.263 PM    07-JUN-04 09.00.12.529 PM        1
    790 07-JUN-04 09.00.12.529 PM    07-JUN-04 10.00.35.827 PM        1
    791 07-JUN-04 10.00.35.827 PM    07-JUN-04 11.01.00.399 PM        1
    792 07-JUN-04 11.01.00.399 PM    08-JUN-04 12.00.22.361 AM        1
    793 08-JUN-04 12.00.22.361 AM    08-JUN-04 01.00.45.758 AM        1
    794 08-JUN-04 01.00.45.758 AM    08-JUN-04 02.00.07.728 AM        1
    795 08-JUN-04 02.00.07.728 AM    08-JUN-04 03.00.31.091 AM        1
    796 08-JUN-04 03.00.31.091 AM    08-JUN-04 04.00.55.874 AM        1
    797 08-JUN-04 04.00.55.874 AM    08-JUN-04 05.00.17.890 AM        1
    798 08-JUN-04 05.00.17.890 AM    08-JUN-04 06.00.41.257 AM        1
    799 08-JUN-04 06.00.41.257 AM    08-JUN-04 07.00.03.188 AM        1
    800 08-JUN-04 07.00.03.188 AM    08-JUN-04 08.00.26.550 AM        1
```

Figure 9.7 – *List of AWR snapshots that can be used for a baseline*

Snapshots

Photographic snapshots are good souvenirs from a trip and help vacationers remember the highlights of a good vacation. AWR snapshots also make good souvenirs with which DBAs can remember the issues that have come up in databases. Snapshots are the way that the AWR keeps track of the issues that are causing performance problems. When talking about baselines in the previous section, the script *awr_list_snaps.sql* was used to show what snapshots are available. It is now time to discover how the snapshots are taken, how the frequency of snapshots is controlled, and the length of time snapshots are stored before they are purged.

By default, these snapshots are taken once every hour and kept for seven days. The *dbms_workload_repository.modify_snapshot_settings* procedure allows the DBA to change these defaults. In an earlier section about STATSPACK, one of the issues mentioned was the determination of a schedule to follow in order to capture granular-enough data without overloading the system with the snapshot activity. AWR is very similar to STATSPACK in this regard. Many DBAs will find one hour snapshots adequate for some systems, but troubleshooting an active database with a critical performance problem will require a more frequent snapshot interval.

Earlier, information was presented on the settings for the frequency and retention of snapshots. The *dba_hist_wr_control* table is the location for these parameters. The following script, *awr_settings.sql*, will show the settings for the current database as shown in figure 9.8 below.

🖫 awr_settings.sql

```
-- ****************************************************
-- Copyright © 2003 by Rampant TechPress
-- This script is free for non-commercial purposes
-- with no warranties.  Use at your own risk.
--
-- To license this script for a commercial purpose,
-- contact info@rampant.cc
-- ****************************************************

/* awr_settings.sql */
column snap_interval format a25
column retention      format a25

select
   snap_interval,
   retention
from
   dba_hist_wr_control;
```

```
SQL> @awr_settings.sql

SNAP_INTERVAL                RETENTION
------------------------     ------------------
+00000 01:00:00.0            +00007 00:00:00.0
```

Figure 9.8 – *Checking AWR Frequency and Retention Settings*

Figure 9.8 clearly indicates that the database in question is configured to take hourly snapshots by the 1 in the hour's position in the SNAP_INTERVAL column and to keep them for seven days per the 7 in the day's position in the RETENTION column. Since this script was run on database with a vanilla install, it appears that the default for the AWR is, in fact, for the snapshots to be taken every 60 minutes.

If these values are not what ideal for the database in question, they can easily be changed. This is done using the *dbms_workload_repository.modify_snapshot_settings* procedure. If the length of the name is bothersome, be thankful it is one less acronym that needs to be remembered. The syntax for this procedure is:

```
DBMS_WORKLOAD_REPOSITORY.MODIFY_SNAPSHOT_SETTINGS(
    retention    IN  NUMBER DEFAULT NULL,
    interval     IN  NUMBER DEFAULT NULL,
    dbid         IN  NUMBER DEFAULT NULL);
```

The numeric values for retention and interval are to be given in minutes. The default for both values is NULL. When NULL is specified for either value, it leaves the current setting unchanged. If dbid is omitted or set to NULL, the procedure will use the current and local dbid. To make things easier, there is a script that calls this procedure and prompts the user for the first two parameters. This script, *awr_settings_change.sql*, leaves off the dbid and prompts the user for a retention value with a bit of helpful advice.

🖫 awr_settings_change.sql

```
--  ****************************************************
--  Copyright © 2003 by Rampant TechPress
--  This script is free for non-commercial purposes
--  with no warranties.  Use at your own risk.
--
--  To license this script for a commercial purpose,
--  contact info@rampant.cc
--  ****************************************************

/* awr_change_settings.sql */
accept retention_minutes prompt "Enter retention in minutes (10080=7
days)"

BEGIN
  DBMS_WORKLOAD_REPOSITORY.MODIFY_SNAPSHOT_SETTINGS(
      retention => &retention_minutes,
      interval => &interval_minutes
      );
END;
/
@awr_settings.sql
```

In Figure 9.9, instead of entering the number of hours to set the retention to 14 days, a simple math formula is used that makes setting virtually any retention period easy. Simply remember that the setting is in minutes. In the example below, 60 was entered for the number of minutes in an hour, 24 for the number of hours in a day and 14 for 14 days' worth of snapshots. Note that 20160 could also have been entered directly. An additional feature of this script is that it displays the new settings after making the change using the *awr_settings.sql* script introduced earlier this chapter.

```
SQL> @awr_change_settings.sql
Enter retention in minutes (10080=7 days) 60*24*14
old    3:         retention => &retention_minutes,
new    3:         retention => 60*24*14,
Enter value for interval_minutes: 30
old    4:         interval => &interval_minutes
new    4:         interval => 30

PL/SQL procedure successfully completed.


SNAP_INTERVAL                      RETENTION
------------------------      ------------------------
+00000 00:30:00.0             +00014 00:00:00.0
```

Figure 9.9 – *AWR Settings: Changing Interval and Retention*

This script makes it simpler to change the retention, but there are relatively few times when this should be done. In general, the DBA should determine what frequency and retention periods make the most sense for the specific database and situation. In some cases, the DBA may be content with hourly snapshots and seven days' worth of history.

To further implement the self-tuning database, it might be a good idea to vary the retention and frequency of the AWR snapshots based on database load or some criteria by which the DBA determines how busy the database is. The frequencies could be shortened when there are problems and lengthened when the problems are all under control.

When troubleshooting a problem that happens less than once a week, DBAs may want to keep history around a bit longer. If the problem is not readily apparent with the hourly frequency because the data about the problem is lumped in with the rest of the work going on over the whole hour, the DBA may want a more frequent snapshot until the issue is resolved. Anytime these settings are changed, the DBA must be sure to revisit space allocation to make sure that the space will not run out so that data collections are not missed due to lack of space.

Conclusion

This chapter covers two of the more important new additions to Oracle10g: Active Session History (ASH) and the Automatic Workload Repository (AWR). These are important features for many reasons. Some of the important details presented in this chapter are:

- ASH maintains a sample of data about sessions that are currently active.

- ASH provides information for the AWR.

- The AWR provides a built-in system for storing data that is similar to STATSPACK in earlier versions.

- The AWR is the foundation for many of the self-tuning features in Oracle10g.

The next chapter will present some of the self-tuning features that are available as part of the Automatic Database Diagnostic Monitor (ADDM).

Automatic Database Diagnostic Monitor

Introduction

In the continued pursuit of making database administration so simple a child could do it, Oracle has introduced number of features designed to automate different administrative functions. Of these, one of the most significant is the Automatic Database Diagnostic Monitor, which is generally referred to by its acronym, ADDM.

"I've heard that Oracle10g can be administered by a 12-year old. Could you please set up some interviews?"

The Automatic Workload Repository (AWR) was covered in the previous chapter. Its function is to automatically collect data that previously required a DBA to install and manage the data collected by STATSPACK. The data that AWR collects is used by many of the components of the ADDM. In fact, every time an AWR snapshot is taken, ADDM does an analysis of the result and current history in the AWR.

The analysis done by ADDM not only includes the problem areas that could be identified in STATSPACK, like top SQL, I/O and parse issues, but also can help identify excessive logon and logoff activity, lock contention, and checkpointing issues. The results of this analysis can be reviewed by looking at tables in the AWR or by using Enterprise Manager (EM). Since EM is a topic unto itself, the focus will be on reviewing these results in the AWR tables.

Methodology

Since the focus of this book is using the Wait Interface and Wait Events to resolve performance problems, it is important to review the methodology that ADDM uses for identifying resolutions to problems. Looking at the ADDM information for tuning allows it to be viewed from several different perspectives:

- Top SQL statements
- Top sessions
- CPU/Wait times

While there may be times when other perspectives have merit, the focus will be on the CPU and wait time approach. Wait information is grouped by wait classes. These classes are groupings of waits by areas of commonality. For example, *db file scattered read* and *db file sequential read* are both part of the I/O class.

The goal of the analysis that ADDM performs is to minimize the metric called DB time. DB time is the total amount of time spent by the database server on user requests. It includes wait time and CPU time of all non-idle user sessions. DB time is displayed in the *v$sess_time_model* and *v$sys_time_model* views containing data for individual sessions and system rollup numbers respectively.

This metric is cumulative, that is it continues to grow as long as the session is connected for *v$sess_time_model*, or as long as the instance has been running for *v$sys_time_model*. This means that a particular value for DB time is irrelevant unless used in comparison to an earlier or later value.

Components

ADDM gathers data and issues alerts about performance issues. The following sections introduce several components that make use of the data gathered by the AWR.

Data Dictionary Objects

The data dictionary objects will be examined first. They will be briefly introduced with regard to their purpose, and then their use will be demonstrated.

The *dba_advisor_objects* view displays information about all database objects currently referenced by the advisors. Each row in this view pertains to a specific advisor tuning object. Figure 10.1 shows the structure of this view.

```
SQL> desc dba_advisor_objects
 Name                     Null?    Type
 ----------------------   -------- ---------------
 OWNER                             VARCHAR2(30)
 OBJECT_ID                NOT NULL NUMBER
 TYPE                              VARCHAR2(64)
 TYPE_ID                  NOT NULL NUMBER
 TASK_ID                  NOT NULL NUMBER
 TASK_NAME                         VARCHAR2(30)
 ATTR1                             VARCHAR2(4000)
 ATTR2                             VARCHAR2(4000)
 ATTR3                             VARCHAR2(4000)
 ATTR4                             CLOB
 ATTR5                             VARCHAR2(4000)
```

Figure 10.1 – *Structure of dba_advisor_objects*

Figure 10.2 shows a portion of the output from *show_addm_objects.sql* which is a sample of data contained in *dba_advisor_objects*. This script is useful to obtain a better idea of the information contained in this view. However, example will be provided later that will show how to use the *object_id* in this view to relate these objects with advisor recommendations, findings, and actions. This example focuses on SQL objects in which *attr4* contains the SQL command in question. Additional field may be included for different types of analysis.

🖫 **show_addm_objects.sql**

```
-- *************************************************
-- Copyright © 2003 by Rampant TechPress
-- This script is free for non-commercial purposes
-- with no warranties.  Use at your own risk.
--
-- To license this script for a commercial purpose,
-- contact info@rampant.cc
-- *************************************************

/* show_addm_objects.sql */
/* list objects that have been reference by an advisor */
set linesize      132
column attr4      format a50 WRAP
column type       format a15 WRAP
column task_name  format a25 WRAP
column object_id  format 99999 head OBJ|ID


select
```

```
   object_id,
   type,
   task_name,
   attr4
from
   dba_advisor_objects;
```

```
OBJ
 ID TYPE            TASK_NAME               ATTR4
---- --------------- ----------------------- -------------------------------------------------
  4 SQL             TASK_1268               SELECT MOD(SUM(TIME_WAITED),9) FROM V$SYSTEM_EVENT
  3 SQL             TASK_1268               SELECT MOD(SUM(TIME_WAITED),6) FROM V$SYSTEM_EVENT
  2 SQL             TASK_1268               SELECT MOD(SUM(TIME_WAITED),4) FROM V$SYSTEM_EVENT
  1 SQL             TASK_1268               SELECT MOD(SUM(TIME_WAITED),9) FROM V$SYSTEM_EVENT
  7 SQL             ADDM:1345855919_1_1488  INSERT INTO HITS VALUES (SYSDATE,:B3 ,:B2 ,:B1 )
  6 SQL             ADDM:1345855919_1_1488  SELECT MOD(SUM(TIME_WAITED),6) FROM V$SYSTEM_EVENT
  5 SQL             ADDM:1345855919_1_1488  SELECT MOD(SUM(TIME_WAITED),4) FROM V$SYSTEM_EVENT
  4 SQL             ADDM:1345855919_1_1488  SELECT MOD(SUM(TIME_WAITED),9) FROM V$SYSTEM_EVENT
  3 SQL             ADDM:1345855919_1_1488  SELECT MOD(SUM(TIME_WAITED),6) FROM V$SYSTEM_EVENT
  2 SQL             ADDM:1345855919_1_1488  SELECT MOD(SUM(TIME_WAITED),4) FROM V$SYSTEM_EVENT
  1 SQL             ADDM:1345855919_1_1488  SELECT MOD(SUM(TIME_WAITED),9) FROM V$SYSTEM_EVENT
  7 SQL             ADDM:1345855919_1_1487  INSERT INTO HITS VALUES (SYSDATE,:B3 ,:B2 ,:B1 )
```

Figure 10.2 – *Example of data in dba_advisor_objects*

The data in *dba_advisor_actions* contains information about the actions associated with all recommendations in the database. Each action is specified by the *command* and *attr#* columns. Every different command will use the attribute columns in specific ways. The following query will demonstrate the current advisor recommended actions. This may be overwhelming at first, but by filtering on a specific object_id, it is possible to see the recommendations for a particular query or database object.

🖫 **show_addm_actions.sql**

```
-- ****************************************************
-- Copyright © 2003 by Rampant TechPress
-- This script is free for non-commercial purposes
-- with no warranties.  Use at your own risk.
--
-- To license this script for a commercial purpose,
-- contact info@rampant.cc
-- ****************************************************

/* show_addm_actions.sql */
/* list actions that have been recommended by an advisor */

set linesize      132
column message    format a60 WRAP
column command    format a15 WRAP
```

```
column task_name format a25 WRAP
column object_id format 99999 head OBJ|ID
column action_id format 99999 head ACTION|ID

select
   object_id,
   action_id,
   command,
   message
from
   dba_advisor_actions;
```

Figure 10.3 shows some of the general recommendations that are being made for the whole instance, including resizing the *log_buffer* parameter and increasing the number of database writer processes.

```
ACTION
    ID COMMAND         MESSAGE
------ --------------- ---------------------------------------------------------------

     4 ALTER PARAMETER Consider increasing the number of database writers (DBWR) by
                       setting the parameter "db_writer_processes".

     9 ALTER PARAMETER Increase the size of the redo log buffer by setting the valu
                       e of parameter "log_buffer" to 16 M.

     4 ALTER PARAMETER Consider increasing the number of database writers (DBWR) by
                       setting the parameter "db_writer_processes".

     9 ALTER PARAMETER Increase the size of the redo log buffer by setting the valu
                       e of parameter "log_buffer" to 15 M.
```

Figure 10.3 – *Example of data in dba_advisor_actions*

The *dba_advisor_findings* view provides all the findings and symptoms that any advisors have discovered along with the specific recommendation to resolve them. Figure 10.4 shows the structure of this view.

```
SQL> desc dba_advisor_findings
 Name                       Null?      Type
 ----------------------     --------   --------------
 OWNER                                 VARCHAR2(30)
 TASK_ID                    NOT NULL   NUMBER
 TASK_NAME                             VARCHAR2(30)
 FINDING_ID                 NOT NULL   NUMBER
 TYPE                                  VARCHAR2(11)
 PARENT                     NOT NULL   NUMBER
 OBJECT_ID                             NUMBER
 IMPACT_TYPE                           VARCHAR2(4000)
 IMPACT                                NUMBER
 MESSAGE                               VARCHAR2(4000)
 MORE_INFO                             VARCHAR2(4000)
```

Figure 10.4 – *Structure of dba_advisor_findings*

The *task_id* field can be used to gather more information about a specific task. These findings can be in one of four categories as shows in the *type* field:

- Problem

- Symptom

- Error

- Information

These categorizations provide a triage area to look at the PROBLEM items first. These are the items where the *type* is set to the string PROBLEM. A DBA allowing ADDM to advise on database performance issues will, ideally, work their way down to review and address the INFORMATION items.

The script *show_addm_findings.sql* will list the items in the PROBLEM category. Figure 10.5 is a sample of the output from this script when dealing with a CPU bottleneck issue.

🖫 show_addm_findings.sql

```
-- ****************************************************
-- Copyright © 2003 by Rampant TechPress
-- This script is free for non-commercial purposes
-- with no warranties.  Use at your own risk.
--
-- To license this script for a commercial purpose,
-- contact info@rampant.cc
-- ****************************************************

/* show_addm_findings.sql */
set lines 132
set pages 99
column task_name     format a23
column impact_type   format a40
column message       format a100 WRAP

select
   task_name,
   type,
   impact_type,
   impact,
   message
from
   dba_advisor_findings
where
   message not like 'There was no significant database%'
and
   type = 'PROBLEM'
and
   impact > 1000
order by
   impact;
```

```
TASK_NAME               TYPE         IMPACT_TYPE                              IMPACT
----------------------- ----------- ---------------------------------------- ----------
MESSAGE
------------------------------------------------------------------------------------------------
ADDM:1345855919_1_1487  PROBLEM      Database time in microseconds.           2056415701
SQL statements consuming significant database time were found.

ADDM:1345855919_1_915   PROBLEM      Database time in microseconds.           2073145578
Time spent on the CPU by the instance was responsible for a substantial part of database time.

ADDM:1345855919_1_912   PROBLEM      Database time in microseconds.           2077101003
Time spent on the CPU by the instance was responsible for a substantial part of database time.

TASK_1268               PROBLEM      Database time in microseconds.           2146046777
Host CPU was a bottleneck and the instance was consuming 83% of the host CPU. All wait times will be
 inflated by wait for CPU.

ADDM:1345855919_1_1487  PROBLEM      Database time in microseconds.           2146046777
Host CPU was a bottleneck and the instance was consuming 83% of the host CPU. All wait times will be
 inflated by wait for CPU.
```

Figure 10.5 – *Example of ADDM findings*

dba_advisor_recommendations displays the results of completed diagnostic tasks with recommendations for the problems identified in each run. The recommendations should be looked at and sorted by the value in the *rank* column, as this relays the magnitude of the problem for the recommendation. The *benefit* column contains the projected benefit that will result for the system if this recommendation is followed. Figure 10.6 is the structure of this view and figure 10.7 provides sample data found in its key fields.

```
SQL> desc dba_advisor_recommendations
 Name                    Null?    Type
 ---------------------   -------- --------------
 OWNER                            VARCHAR2(30)
 REC_ID                  NOT NULL NUMBER
 TASK_ID                 NOT NULL NUMBER
 TASK_NAME                        VARCHAR2(30)
 FINDING_ID                       NUMBER
 TYPE                             VARCHAR2(30)
 RANK                             NUMBER
 PARENT_REC_IDS                   VARCHAR2(4000)
 BENEFIT_TYPE                     VARCHAR2(4000)
 BENEFIT                          NUMBER
 ANNOTATION_STATUS                VARCHAR2(11)
```

Figure 10.6 – *Structure of dba_advisor_recommendations*

```
TASK_NAME                 TYPE                    RANK     BENEFIT
----------------------    --------------------    ----    ----------
ADDM:1345855919_1_717     DB Configuration          0      6731324
ADDM:1345855919_1_717     Application Analysis      1      6691190
ADDM:1345855919_1_717     SQL Tuning                1     48339726
ADDM:1345855919_1_717     Application Analysis      1     26813493
ADDM:1345855919_1_717     SQL Tuning                1     83497382
ADDM:1345855919_1_717     SQL Tuning                2     47805198
ADDM:1345855919_1_717     SQL Tuning                2     79128165
ADDM:1345855919_1_717     SQL Tuning                3     44425078
ADDM:1345855919_1_717     SQL Tuning                3     64009592
ADDM:1345855919_1_717     SQL Tuning                4     19342584
```

Figure 10.7 – *Sample data from dba_advisor_recommendations*

The values identified above in the *task_name* field can be followed with information from the *dba_advisor_findings*. For more details on implementing the recommendations; look at the recommendations for a specific *task_name* with a script like *show_addm_recommendations.sql*.

🖫 show_addm_recommendations.sql

```
-- **************************************************
-- Copyright © 2003 by Rampant TechPress
-- This script is free for non-commercial purposes
-- with no warranties.  Use at your own risk.
--
-- To license this script for a commercial purpose,
-- contact info@rampant.cc
-- **************************************************

/* show_addm_recommendations.sql */
set lines 132
set pages 99
column task_name    format a25
column type         format a25
column rank         format 9999
column benefit      format 999999999

select
   task_name,
   type,
   rank,
   benefit
from
   dba_advisor_recommendations
where
   task_name = '&task_name'
order by
   task_name,
   rank;
```

After getting this high-level view from *dba_advisor_recommendations*, the next step is to gather more detailed information by looking at the *dba_advisor_findings* view. *dba_advisor_rationale* is the way to understand why a specific recommendation is being made. This is an important step because if the reasoning behind a given recommendation does not apply in this environment or situation, it should not be followed. It is up to the DBA to make certain this analysis takes place. If the DBA is not fully aware of the specifics around the application or data usage, they may need to work with application developers or business users to make an informed choice.

```
SQL> desc dba_advisor_rationale
 Name                       Null?    Type
 -------------------------- -------- --------------
 OWNER                               VARCHAR2(30)
 TASK_ID            NOT NULL NUMBER
 TASK_NAME                           VARCHAR2(30)
 REC_ID                              NUMBER
 RATIONALE_ID       NOT NULL NUMBER
 IMPACT_TYPE                         VARCHAR2(4000)
 IMPACT                              NUMBER
 MESSAGE                             VARCHAR2(4000)
 OBJECT_ID                           NUMBER
 TYPE                                VARCHAR2(30)
 ATTR1                               VARCHAR2(4000)
 ATTR2                               VARCHAR2(4000)
 ATTR3                               VARCHAR2(4000)
 ATTR4                               VARCHAR2(4000)
 ATTR5                               CLOB
```

Figure 10.8 – *Structure of dba_advisor_rationale*

Figure 10.8 shows the structure of *dba_advisor_rationale*. The main fields of interest are *impact_type*, *impact*, and *message*. Figure 10.9 shows examples of the rationale that is provided for several recommendations for these tasks. *show_addm_rationale.sql* is a script that can be used that will prompt for a *task_name* and will provide information in the same format as this figure.

```
TASK_NAME              IMPACT_TYPE                      IMPACT MESSAGE
---------------------- ------------------------------ -------------- ------------------------------------------------------------
ADDM:1345855919_1_717  Database time in microseconds.            0 SQL statements with PLAN_HASH_VALUE 1311921166 were fou
                                                                    nd to be using literals. Look in V$SQL for examples of
                                                                    such SQL statements.

ADDM:1345855919_1_910  Database time in microseconds.  112,527,634 The SQL statement with SQL_ID "7ahwsg16zds94" was found
                                                                    waiting for "log file switch completion" wait event.

ADDM:1345855919_1_910  Database time in microseconds.  331,744,343 The average size of writes to the online redo log files
                                                                    was 86 K and the average time per write was 0 millisec
                                                                    onds.

ADDM:1345855919_1_910  Database time in microseconds.   82,302,692 The SQL statement with SQL_ID "7ahwsg16zds94" spent sig
                                                                    nificant time waiting for User I/O on the hot object.

ADDM:1345855919_1_911  Database time in microseconds.  111,603,104 The SQL statement with SQL_ID "7ahwsg16zds94" was found
                                                                    waiting for "log file switch completion" wait event.
```

Figure 10.9 – *Example of dba_advisor_rationale data*

🖫 show_addm_rationale.sql

```
-- ***************************************************
-- Copyright © 2003 by Rampant TechPress
-- This script is free for non-commercial purposes
-- with no warranties.  Use at your own risk.
--
-- To license this script for a commercial purpose,
-- contact info@rampant.cc
-- ***************************************************

/* show_addm_rationale.sql */
column MESSAGE format a55
column IMPACT_TYPE format a30
column IMPACT format 9,999,999,999
select
   task_name,
   impact_type,
   impact,
   message
from
   dba_advisor_rationale
where
   task_name = '&task_name';
```

The view *dba_advisor_tasks* provides basic information such as the task id, task name, and date created for current tasks. The full structure can be viewed in Figure 10.10.

```
SQL> desc dba_advisor_tasks
 Name                     Null?       Type
 --------------------     --------    --------------
 OWNER                                VARCHAR2(30)
 TASK_ID                  NOT NULL    NUMBER
 TASK_NAME                            VARCHAR2(30)
 DESCRIPTION                          VARCHAR2(256)
 ADVISOR_NAME                         VARCHAR2(30)
 CREATED                  NOT NULL    DATE
 LAST_MODIFIED            NOT NULL    DATE
 PARENT_TASK_ID                       NUMBER
 PARENT_REC_ID                        NUMBER
 EXECUTION_START                      DATE
 EXECUTION_END                        DATE
 STATUS                               VARCHAR2(11)
 STATUS_MESSAGE                       VARCHAR2(4000)
 PCT_COMPLETION_TIME                  NUMBER
 PROGESS_METRIC                       NUMBER
 METRIC_UNITS                         VARCHAR2(64)
 ACTIVITY_COUNTER                     NUMBER
 RECOMMENDATION_COUNT                 NUMBER
 ERROR_MESSAGE                        VARCHAR2(4000)
 SOURCE                               VARCHAR2(30)
 HOW_CREATED                          VARCHAR2(30)
 READ_ONLY                            VARCHAR2(5)
 ADVISOR_ID               NOT NULL    NUMBER
```

Figure 10.10 – *Structure of dba_advisor_tasks*

dba_advisor_tasks also maintains the status of each task. The status is set to one of the following six values:

INITIAL - Initial state of the task; no recommendations are present since nothing has been done.

EXECUTING - Task is currently running.

INTERRUPTED - Task analysis was interrupted by the user. If recommendations are present, they can be viewed and reported on at this time.

COMPLETED - Task successfully completed the analysis operation. Recommendation data can be viewed and reported.

CANCELLED – Task has been cancelled.

FATAL ERROR - An error occurred during the analysis operation. If recommendations are available, they can be examined and reported on at this time.

Something that may be beneficial when added to the database monitoring procedures is a routine check to see if any tasks have a status of FATAL ERROR. Upon finding any, determine why the error occurred.

```
                                                                                    ADVISOR
TASK_NAME               DESCRIPTION                                                 NAME
----------------------- -------------------------------------------------------     -------
STATUS                  ERROR_MESSAGE
----------------------- -------------------------------------------------------
ADDM:1345855919_1_740   ADDM auto run: snapshots [739, 740],  instance 1,  database id 1345855919        ADDM
FATAL ERROR             Either the start snapshot 739 or the end snapshot 740 is incomplete or missing key statistics.

ADDM:1345855919_1_691   ADDM auto run: snapshots [690, 691],  instance 1,  database id 1345855919        ADDM
FATAL ERROR             Either the start snapshot 690 or the end snapshot 691 is incomplete or missing key statistics.

ADDM:1345855919_1_788   ADDM auto run: snapshots [787, 788],  instance 1,  database id 1345855919        ADDM
FATAL ERROR             Either the start snapshot 787 or the end snapshot 788 is incomplete or missing key statistics.

ADDM:1345855919_1_812   ADDM auto run: snapshots [811, 812],  instance 1,  database id 1345855919        ADDM
FATAL ERROR             Either the start snapshot 811 or the end snapshot 812 is incomplete or missing key statistics.
```

Figure 10.11 – *Sample errors in dba_advisor_tasks*

💾 **show_addm_tasks_in_error.sql**

```
-- ************************************************
-- Copyright © 2003 by Rampant TechPress
-- This script is free for non-commercial purposes
-- with no warranties.  Use at your own risk.
--
-- To license this script for a commercial purpose,
-- contact info@rampant.cc
-- ************************************************

/* show_addm_tasks_in_error.sql */
column ADVISOR_NAME    format a10 WRAP head ADVISOR|NAME
column DESCRIPTION     format a40
column STATUS_MESSAGE  format a40

select
   task_name,
   description,
   advisor_name,
   status,
   status_message
from
   dba_advisor_tasks
where
   status like '%ERROR%';
```

Figure 10.11 shows the output of the script *show_addm_tasks_in_error.sql* that could be use for this purpose. In these examples, there was apparently a problem with the AWR (Automatic Workload Repository) during a number of snapshots. This made the report the ADDM advisor tried to run unsuccessful. If the problem with the AWR has been resolved, disregard these errors. The recommendations will "age-out" just like the AWR data it is created from.

Another query on this table would quickly provide the start and end times for any tasks that were not completed successfully. This would allow fine-tuning of the above script to only report errors where the *execution_end* timestamp was within the past day.

dba_advisor_log contains the current task information, such as status, progress, error messages, and execution times. To monitor for errors in this process, there are several factors to look at to determine if errors had occurred. One way might be where the *status_message* contains the word "ERROR". Another might be if *execution_start* is more than five minutes ago and *execution_end* is null. The structure of this view is shown below in Figure 10.12

```
SQL> desc dba_advisor_log
 Name                     Null?      Type
 ----------------------   --------   ---------------
 OWNER                               VARCHAR2 (30)
 TASK_ID                  NOT NULL   NUMBER
 TASK_NAME                           VARCHAR2 (30)
 EXECUTION_START                     DATE
 EXECUTION_END                       DATE
 STATUS                              VARCHAR2 (11)
 STATUS_MESSAGE                      VARCHAR2 (4000)
 PCT_COMPLETION_TIME                 NUMBER
 PROGESS_METRIC                      NUMBER
 METRIC_UNITS                        VARCHAR2 (64)
 ACTIVITY_COUNTER                    NUMBER
 RECOMMENDATION_COUNT                NUMBER
 ERROR_MESSAGE                       VARCHAR2 (4000)
```

Figure 10.12 – *Structure of dba_advisor_log*

The *status* field can contain one of six status conditions. These conditions are the same ones found in *dba_advisor_tasks*. Any query that works using the *status* field in *dba_advisor_tasks* view will work in the *dba_advisor_log* view. This is due to the fact that all fields found in *dba_advisor_tasks* are also found in *dba_advisor_log*. Moreover, the values in the fields will be the same since both views are built from *wri$_adv_tasks*. Effectively, this means that any information desired from *dba_advisor_log*, can be obtained from *dba_advisor_tasks*.

Reports

Just as Oracle provided a basic script for a STATSPACK report (*spreport.sql*), Oracle has also provided a script to gather ADDM information (*addmrpt.sql*). This script provides a way to review the data that the AWR has gathered and the results of the analysis that ADDM has done. This script is located at *$ORACLE_HOME/rdbms/admin*. There is also a built in package that is provided to access the ADDM features. This package is called *dbms_advisor* and contains many useful procedures that allow for viewing and setting of the values that drive the advisor analysis.

NOTE: Any user can execute these scripts and procedures, as long as they have been granted the ADVISOR privilege.

Figure 10.13 below shows a sample run of the *addmrpt* report.

```
DETAILED ADDM REPORT FOR TASK 'TASK_1268' WITH ID 1268
--------------------------------------------------------

          Analysis Period: 25-JUN-2004 from 21:30:04 to 22:00:48
       Database ID/Instance: 1345855919/1
    Database/Instance Names: TOY10/TOY10
                  Host Name: mark
           Database Version: 10.1.0.2.0
             Snapshot Range: from 1486 to 1487
              Database Time: 2146 seconds
      Average Database Load: 1.2 active sessions


~~~~~~~~~~~~~~~~~~~~~~~~~~~~~~~~~~~~~~~~~~~~~~~~~~~~~~~~~~~~~~~~~~~~~~~~~~~~~~~~


FINDING 1: 100% impact (2146 seconds)
-------------------------------------
Host CPU was a bottleneck and the instance was consuming 83% of the host CPU.
All wait times will be inflated by wait for CPU.

   RECOMMENDATION 1: Host Configuration, 100% benefit (2146 seconds)
      ACTION: Consider adding more CPUs to the host or increasing the number
         of instances serving the database.

   RECOMMENDATION 2: SQL Tuning, 27% benefit (590 seconds)
      ACTION: Run SQL Tuning Advisor on the SQL statement with SQL_ID
         "cdctb4b17vbs0".
```

Figure 10.13 – *Sample run of the addmrpt report*

The header of this report contains information on the period of time when this report was run, as well as information on the database and instance for which it was run. The body of the report is presented as a series of *findings*. Each finding is presented with an overall bottleneck report, and one or more *recommendations* on how to ease that bottleneck. Each recommendation displays an estimated benefit available by following the said recommendation.

The first finding is that the CPU is the biggest bottleneck. The first recommendation is to add more CPUs or add instances to support this load. In this case, adding more instances would not resolve the problem since the average load, as shown by the header information, is only 1.2 sessions. Adding CPUs would only enhance performance if the busy session was able to take advantage of the parallelism offered by an increased CPU count.

If this is a batch job, there is likely some serious redesign that will be required to support this approach since simply putting more CPUs in a machine will not necessarily improve performance for a given user.

Advisors

ADDM can identify the SQL statements that fall into the high-load category based on the quantity of resources that they utilize. The categorization of SQL statements as high-load is dependent on several factors including the available CPU and memory resources of the host. More importantly, it is categorized based on relative resource usage. A SQL statement making 10,000 logical I/O's (LIO) on one system may be the norm and not considered high-load; whereas, on another system, a 5,000 LIO statement might be the top offender.

After ADDM identifies the candidate high-load SQL statements, the next step is to determine if they are using resources optimally. In most cases, these statements will reduce the quantity of resources they require with proper tuning. In the past, the available options to conduct proper tuning were hands-on tuning or third-party applications.

The hands-on tuning involved testing different hints, adding indexes, and rewriting SQL, according to one expert's latest white paper to avoid the latest item on the Bad SQL "Top 10 List".

- Implementing hash-joins (or avoiding them).

- Implementing correlated subqueries (or avoiding them).

- Listing the joined tables in order by number of rows retrieved.

This list could go on, but the idea was clear – follow the latest checklist for SQL tuning and hope it made the bad SQL run better.

The tool sets and third party applications often made this hands-on task much easier by automating the more common solutions and testing via explain plans whether the cost was decreased. For the most part, there was no additional "thinking" behind the tool, so the DBA still had to evaluate the analysis and determine which modifications made sense. Additionally, new ideas in tuning took time in getting implemented into the knowledgebase in these tools.

Now, Oracle has created the SQL Tuning Advisor, which claims to make SQL tuning much easier and more efficient. It adds to the features in the previously mentioned tools, but also provides a projected improvement from following the advice. The areas where the SQL Tuning Advisor works are discussed next.

The first area to mention is the detection of stale or missing statistics. The cost-based optimizer is only as good as the statistics on the tables and indexes. Looking for objects without statistics has been an item on many DBA checklists, but Oracle adds this to the Tuning Advisor. The Tuning Advisor has a method to determine not only whether the statistics are there, but also claims to determine whether they are stale. Missing and stale statistics should be less common with the addition of Automatic Statistics Gathering, introduced in 10g.

Another area that the SQL Tuning Advisor looks at is execution plan optimization. When this capability is enabled, the CBO collects information about SQL statements. This information includes historical run time, cardinality, and selectivity. The CBO takes advantage of this information to continue to enhance execution plans until an optimal plan is found. Since the SQL

Profile that contains this information is kept in the data dictionary, it assists in generating efficient execution plans without any changes to the application code.

The SQL Tuning Advisor also performs access path tuning. The recommendations may include new indexes or running the SQL Access Advisor. The SQL Access Advisor uses information stored in *dba_advisor_sqla_wk_map* to make recommendations for more efficient methods to access data. Implementation and use of SQL Access Advisor is a separate topic and outside of the scope of this book.

SQL reconstruction is another way the SQL Tuning Advisor can recommend performance improvements. The recommendations it makes are SQL that *most likely* will produce the same result set, but should always be checked by someone familiar with the data and application to confirm identical function.

While these are important tools in the toolbox of any DBA, they are not the first step when using the Wait Event approach. Simply finding the worst SQL statements and making them more effective may not benefit the user community. It is important to make certain the improvements being made matter to the business in order to maintain the satisfaction of the customers. These advisors from Oracle can help in certain cases, and in some situations may provide an adequate level of performance. In many other cases, over-reliance on these tools will hinder the ability of the technical staff to solve critical business problems.

While the Advisors are most visibly GUI and integrated into Enterprise Manager (EM), the *dbms_sqltune* package makes it possible to accomplish the same functions from the command line. Whether using EM or command line with packages or even direct queries against certain data dictionary objects, it is important to recall that many of these features are additional cost items. In many cases, the additional cost may not be justified if a reasonably experienced DBA is available.

Conclusions

This last chapter discussed ADDM, the Automatic Database Diagnostic Monitor. Conceptually, ADDM is a leap forward in database management. The ideas and technologies that are implemented by ADDM represent a significant advance in what a database management system is designed to do. Limited testing with this new feature reveals that some ideas are useful and will be immediately beneficial to many DBAs. For example, the SQL Access Advisor will be helpful in quickly providing recommendations for improving performance for SQL statements.

"With ADDM, your database will be running top notch in no time."

On the other hand, the various advisors make many recommendations, and it is still up to the DBA to determine

---

which recommendations to implement. Improperly applied, some recommendations could result in worse performance.

These last few chapters have introduced several new features that have been included in the latest release of Oracle, 10g. This book is not a new features book, so only a few of the more noteworthy additions in the tuning arena will be examined. Some of these are:

- Automatic Workload Repository (AWR)
- Active Session History (ASH)
- Automatic Database Diagnostic Monitor (ADDM)

While these new features have great potential for making an Oracle database easier to manage, there is still much left to be controlled by the DBA. In addition, there will likely be some issues with the initial releases of the advisors. These issues will require oversight to resolve, and an experienced DBA who understands the concepts presented in this book will be well equipped for that challenge. As these issues are resolved and the ADDM functionality improves, it will fall to the proactive DBA to monitor the effectiveness of the ADDM recommendations.

Finally, there will be plenty of opportunities for an experienced DBA working in areas like capacity planning and troubleshooting. Problem resolution will require DBAs with experience both inside and outside of the database. A DBA will need to understand more about networks, operating systems, and storage systems. This knowledge will be needed to work effectively with other groups in supporting the users of the database. Also, with the continued migration to web-based applications, it is likely to be increasingly important for a DBA to work closely with the application developers and designers and the middleware or application server teams.

These changes mean that one skill set in particular will become more critical than ever before. Good communication was once a rare thing in the halls of IT. It will become rare for a DBA to be effective without not only technical skills, but also interpersonal skills and effective communication.

References

This section is intended to help the DBA locate more information. Some of these are on subjects that could not be fully covered in a compact book like this or where more information than was presented might be helpful. Others are just resources that have been helpful and may be of value.

- Dave Moore, Oracle Utilities, Rampant TechPress 2003
- Donald Burleson, *High Performance Tuning With STATSPACK*, Oracle Press 2002
- Anjo Kolk, et al, *Yet Another Performance Profiling Method* (Or YAPP-Method) 1999 Paper, http://www.oraperf.com/whitepapers.html [free registration required]
- Cary Millsap, Optimizing Oracle Performance, O'Reilly 2003
- Gaja Krishna Vaidyanatha, et al, *Oracle Performance Tuning 101*, Oracle Press 2001
- Steve Adams website, www.ixora.com.au
- Jonathan Lewis website, www.jlcomp.demon.co.uk
- Hotsos Enterprises, Ltd, www.hotsos.com
- Oracle Metalink, metalink.oracle.com
- The Oak Table, www.oaktable.net
- Oracle Technology Network, technet.oracle.com
- International Oracle Users Group, www.ioug.org
- Oracle-l mailing list, archive available at www.freelists.org/archives/oracle-l

As much as it might seem helpful to list every resource that has been helpful at one time or another, it would not be practical, as it would span more pages that most readers would read. It would also be out-of-date as soon as this book is printed because new resources appear frequently and others change in value and location. Frequently a search engine is a better resource than a list of web pages or books that might or might not be helpful.

Index

About Stephen Andert

 Stephen Andert has been a database administrator for many years and has been working with Oracle for 5 years. He has worked with various different relational databases for over 12 years. He has been a technical reviewer for several Oracle books from O'Reilly & Associates, authored an article on SQL*Loader tuning and has presented at local and international Oracle user group events.

Stephen is an Oracle8 and Oracle8i Oracle Certified Professional and is currently serving on the Board of AZORA, the Arizona Oracle User Group (www.azora.org).

Easy Oracle 10g Automatic DBA

Oracle10g Automatic Storage, Memory and Diagnostic Features

By: Dr. Arun Kumar R.

ISBN 0-9745993-6-0
Retail Price $27.95 / £17.95

This indispensable book shows how a non-Oracle person can quickly install and configure Oracle database 10g for automatic database administration. In less than a day, you can have a complete ready-to-use Oracle database.

Written by one of the world's leading Oracle technology experts, Professor Kumar targets his insights into this highly pragmatic book. This book explains how to use the powerful Oracle 10g automatic features for simple database administration. It has complete coverage for 10g Automatic Storage Management (ASM), 10g Automatic Workload Repository (AWR), Automatic Database Diagnostic Monitor (ADDM), Automatic SGA Management (ASM) and the SQL Tuning Advisor.

For practicing Oracle professionals, this book has a special "for gurus" section at the end of each chapter where Dr. Kumar explains the new Oracle10g v$ views and exposes the internal mechanisms behind these automatic tuning and configuration tools.

http://www.rampant-books.com

Oracle Dataguard

Standby Database Failover Handbook

By: Bipul Kumar

ISBN 0-9745993-8-7
Retail Price $27.95 / £19.95

This book is an essential guide for planning a disaster recovery strategy. Covering all areas of disaster recovery, standby database and automatic Oracle failover, this book explains how the use of Oracle10g Data Guard provides a comprehensive solution for disaster recovery. This book covers all aspects of Oracle Data Guard in detail and provides an overview of the latest Data Guard features in Oracle10g.

Written by a working Oracle DBA, this text covers the concepts and the architecture of standby databases and provides a detailed description of the implementation and management of data guard. Expert tips are revealed for success in configuration and first-time implementation of Data Guard. Advance topics such as "Using RMAN to create Data Guard Configuration" and "Data Guard Broker" have been explained in detail to assist production DBAs managing multiple databases.

http://www.rampant-books.com

Oracle PL/SQL Tuning

Expert Secrets for High Performance Programming

Eric Mortensen & Mike Ault

ISBN 0-9727513-6-X
Retail Price $27.95 / £17.95

PL/SQL tuning makes a huge difference in execution speed. As one of the world's most popular and respected experts, Mike Ault shares his secrets for tuning Oracle PL/SQL.

This indispensable book shows how to hypercharge Oracle applications gaining as much as 30x improvement in execution speed using under-documented code tricks. Packed with working examples, learn how to re-write SQL into PL/SQL and how to use advanced Oracle bulk array processing techniques to achieve super high performance. You can save your company millions of dollars in hardware costs by making your application run at peak efficiency.

Targeted at the Senior Oracle DBA and developer, this advanced book illustrates powerful techniques can make PL/SQL run faster than ever before. Your time savings from a single script is worth the price of this great book.

http://www.rampant-books.com

Oracle Streams

High Speed Replication and Data Sharing

Madhu Tumma

ISBN 0-9745993-5-2
Retail Price $16.95 / £10.95

Oracle Streams is a high-speed tool that allows synchronization of replicated databases across the globe. It is an indispensable feature for any company using Oracle for global eCommerce. A noted and respected Oracle author, Madhu Tumma, shares his secrets for achieving high-speed replication and data sharing. Using proven techniques from mission-critical application, Tumma show the front-line secrets for ensuring success with Oracle Streams. From installation through implementation, Tumma provides step-by-step instruction to ensure success with these powerful Oracle features.

Tumma walks you safely through the myriad of complex Oracle Streams tasks including the set-up of the staging area queue, propagation through data hubs, customized apply functions, rule-based data propagation, Oracle Streams transformation, and lots, lots more. Best of all, Tumma shares working code examples that allow easy management of even the most complex Oracle Streams implementation.

http://www.rampant-books.com

Free!
Oracle 10g Senior DBA Reference Poster

This 24 x 36 inch quick reference includes the important data columns and relationships between the DBA views, allowing you to quickly write complex data dictionary queries.

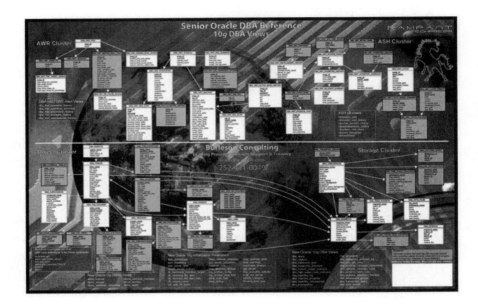

This comprehensive data dictionary reference contains the most important columns from the most important Oracle10g DBA views. Especially useful are the Automated Workload Repository (AWR) and Active Session History (ASH) DBA views.

WARNING - This poster is not suitable for beginners. It is designed for senior Oracle DBAs and requires knowledge of Oracle data dictionary internal structures. You can get your poster at this URL:

www.rampant.cc/poster.htm